KU-571-211

Hamas
A Beginner's Guide

Khaled Hroub

Pluto Press
London • Ann Arbor, MI

First published 2006 by Pluto Press
345 Archway Road, London N6 5AA
and 839 Greene Street, Ann Arbor, MI 48106

www.plutobooks.com

Copyright © Khaled Hroub 2006

The right of Khaled Hroub to be identified as the author of this work has been
asserted by him in accordance with the Copyright, Designs and Patents Act 1988.

British Library Cataloguing in Publication Data
A catalogue record for this book is available from the British Library

ISBN 978 0 74532 590 3 paperback

Library of Congress Cataloging in Publication Data applied for

10 9 8 7 6 5 4 3 2

Designed and produced for Pluto Press by Curran Publishing Services, Norwich
Printed and bound in Canada by Transcontinental Printing

Contents

[v]

CONTENTS

[vi]

Preface

Hamas used to make shocking news the world over by its suicide attacks at the hearts of Israeli cities – unreserved retaliation to the continuous Israeli attacks against Palestinian cities and people. With no less of an impact, Hamas shocked the world in an unexpected way on 25 January 2006 by winning a landslide victory in the elections of the Palestinian Legislative Council (PLC). The PLC, although a quasi-parliament with limited sovereign powers, represents the embodiment of Palestinian political legitimacy in the West Bank and Gaza Strip. By virtue of its victory Hamas formed a government and became the leading force in the national Palestinian struggle for the first time since it was founded in late 1987.

The result of the elections stunned the world. How could it be that a 'terrorist organization' as it is has always been labelled in the West, with a spooky secretive image, as it has been always portrayed in Western media, had emerged as a victorious popular political power? Hamas's main rival had been the secular Fatah movement, which had led the Palestinians for almost half a century almost without interruption. Israel, the United States, Europe, the Arab regimes, the UN and many other regional and international players wanted Fatah to win. Against all odds and enemies Hamas triumphed! The entire world bemoaned, 'What went wrong?'

In fact there was no 'right' against which 'wrong' could be measured in the context of the Palestinian elections. What went wrong, indeed, was the persistent and prevailing misconception of Hamas and the belittling of its power and leverage. Hamas in the eyes of many Westerners, official and lay alike, has always been reduced to a mere 'terrorist group' whose only function is and has been to aimlessly kill Israelis. On the ground in their own country, Hamas has been seen by many Palestinians as a deeply entrenched socio-political and popular force. In Palestinian eyes Hamas had been managing to chart parallel and harmonious paths of both military confrontation against the Israeli occupation, and grass-roots social work, religious and ideological mobilisation and PR networking with other states and movements.

This book sets forth to tell the story of the 'real Hamas', not the misperceived and distorted one. By 'real Hamas' I mean the reality of Hamas as it has been on the ground in all its aspects – debunking any reductionist approach. Yet there is no intention here to provide an apologetic treatise about Hamas. It is up to the reader to shape her or his own opinion on this Palestinian move-ment. The purpose of this book, though, is to provide the basic information and necessary clarifying analysis.

The chapters of the book take the format of questions and answers, which may not seem very familiar. But it is in the inter-est of simplifying what could be seen by many as a complicated issue. Presenting the 'most frequently asked questions' about Hamas (within the Arab/Israeli conflict) and tackling them sepa-rately allows for a more straightforward and accessible read. The chapters are structured in both chronological and thematic fashion starting with the origins of Hamas and ending with the 'new Hamas' (Hamas after the elections), with all other aspects and issues relating to Hamas in between.

Over the past 16 years I have been following the develop-ments of and within Hamas. I have written extensively on its social, political, military and religious aspects. I have published books, chapters in books, journal articles and many other writings trying to understand Hamas and convey my understanding to read-ers. I have interviewed Hamas's leaders and met many of its policy makers. Based on my close knowledge and first hand contact with Hamas people, I have taken the liberty to free the text in this book from footnotes and tiring references. In my other works such referencing and documentation is widely available, if sought.

My own perception of Hamas goes beyond the mere question of being with or against the movement. As a secular person myself, my aspiration is for Palestine, and all other Arab countries for that matter, to be governed by human-made laws. However, I see Hamas as a natural outcome of un-natural, brutal occupational conditions. The radicalism of Hamas should be seen as a completely predictable result of the ongoing Israeli colonial project in Palestine. Palestinians support whichever movement holds the banner of resistance against that occupation and promises to defend the Palestinian rights of freedom and self-determination. At this juncture of history, they see in Hamas the defender of those rights.

Words of gratitude are indeed due at the outset to family, friends and colleagues whose efforts and help make the publication of this book possible. I thank Roger van Zwanenberg of Pluto Books for his encouragement and friendly persistence to have me write this book. I also thank the staff at Pluto Books who put great effort in the production process of the book, Melanie Patrick, Helen Griffiths, Alec Gregory and Susan Curran from Curran Publishing. My sincere thanks go to my Cambridge friend and editor Pam Manix who stood by me chapter by chapter, glued to her computer during all those late nights of writing the book. I also thank Abed al-Juebeh, my dear friend and colleague at al-Jazeera, for his support and help. The ongoing insightful discussions with him, along with his critical and sometimes cynical mind were sources of inspiration for me. The final thanks and love go to my precious small family: Kholoud my wife and friend and my children Laith and Mayce, who as ever endured the little time I've given to them during the writing of this book, yet surrounded me with love, warmth and affection.

Introduction

In January 2006 Hamas stunned the world by winning the democratic elections for the Palestinian Legislative Council of the limited Palestinian Authority in the West Bank and the Gaza Strip. Bringing Hamas into the unprecedented glare of the limelight, this victory shocked many Palestinians, Israel, the United States, Europe and Arab countries. It also left the defeated Palestinian Fatah movement, Hamas's main rival which had led the Palestinian national movement for more than 40 years, completely shattered.

Despite the shock and surprise, Hamas's victory in those elections was in fact almost unavoidable. The cumulative failure over the past years to end a continuing brutal Israeli occupation of Palestinian land and people had only deepened the frustration and radicalism within the Palestinian people. Palestinian frustration and suffering has never ended since the creation of Israel by war in 1948. With British collusion and American support and against the will and interest of the native population, the piece of land that had been known for many hundreds of years as Palestine became Israel. In this war to create Israel the Palestinians lost more than 78 per cent of the land of Palestine, including the western part of their capital Jerusalem. What remained to the Palestinians were two separate pieces of land known as the West Bank (of the Jordan River) adjacent to the country of Jordan, which included a fragment of their old capital city, East Jerusalem, and the Gaza Strip on the Mediterranean bordering the Egyptian Sinai peninsula. As a result of the 1948 war, hundreds of thousands of Palestinians were driven out from their cities and villages to neighbouring countries by Zionist forces. These 'refugees' have become the most intractable problem of the conflict, growing in numbers with their descendants to more than 6 million by the year 2006.

In 1967 Israel launched another successful war, this time not just against the Palestinians but also against all the bordering Arab countries as well. Palestinian losses were nearly complete. With this war Israel occupied the West Bank and the eastern part of Jerusalem, which had been under Jordanian rule, and the Gaza Strip, which had been administered by Egypt since the 1948 war. Israel also invaded Syria's Golan Heights in the north, and Egypt's Sinai desert in the South, and staunchly occupied them all in the name of Israeli security. Yet for the Palestinians the losses were multiple. The Israeli army forced another mass transfer of Palestinians refugees, this time from the West Bank cities and villages to neighbouring countries. Many of the refugees who had been uprooted to the West Bank during the 1948 war were moved on yet again, and with even more new refugees because of the 1967 war. The problem of Palestinian refugees had worsened.

Weakened Arab countries, along with the nascent Palestinian national liberation movement, failed in their military efforts to regain the land they had lost to Israel in 1967. Two years prior to that war, Yasser Arafat and other Palestinian activists in the West Bank and Gaza Strip and neighbouring Arab countries established Fatah, the Palestinian national liberation movement. Fatah declared a no-ideology affiliation and a secular outlook. Around the same time, and with other smaller leftist factions, the Palestine Liberation Organization (PLO) was established as a national umbrella front for the Palestinian struggle, with the clear leadership of Fatah. The goal of the PLO was to 'liberate Palestine': that was to say, the land that had been occupied in the war of 1948 and which had become known as Israel. Yet after the devastating loss of the West Bank and Gaza Strip in 1967, the goal of the PLO had to be reduced. Instead of 'liberating Palestine' it focused on the liberation of only the two more recently lost parts of the land, the West Bank and the Gaza Strip. This goal was seen at this time merely as intermediate phase which would not affect the long-term goal of liberating the entire land of Palestine.

From the mid-1960s to almost the mid-1980s the PLO-led Palestinian national movement embraced armed struggle as the principal strategy to 'liberate Palestine'. Arab weakness coupled with continuous international and Western support of Israel made the Palestinians' mission of liberating their land almost impossible. Achieving no success over decades of struggle, the PLO made two historic concessions by the end of the 1980s. It relinquished its long-term goal – the 'liberation of Palestine' – by recognizing Israel and its right to exist. It also dropped the armed struggle as a strategy, for the sake of a negotiated settlement that hoped to regain the West Bank and the Gaza Strip and establish an independent Palestinian state.

In 1991 the United States convened the Madrid Peace Conference in the aftermath of the first Gulf War and the expulsion of Saddam Hussein's troops from Kuwait. With Arabs everywhere fragmented because of the Iraqi invasion of Kuwait, the ensuing war, and a weakened Palestinian position because the PLO had sided (verbally and politically) with Iraq against the American-led coalition troops, the PLO's negotiating position in Madrid was fragile. Not unexpectedly, the Conference failed to produce a Palestinian/Israeli peace treaty, but succeeded in confirming the historic shift on the side of the PLO towards negotiation instead of armed struggle as its preferred strategy to end the conflict.

In 1993 an initial agreement was reached between the PLO

and Israel, the Oslo Agreement, after months of secret talks in Norway. Endorsed in Washington by the Clinton Administration, the agreement was in theory divided into two phases: a five-year interim phase (essentially meant to explore and test the competence of the Palestinians to peacefully rule themselves and control 'illegal' armed resistance factions) starting in 1994, which if it proved successful would be followed by a second phase of negotiations on a 'final settlement'. The Palestinians were almost evenly divided in response to the Oslo Accords. Those who supported Oslo argued that it was the best deal that the Palestinians could hope to achieve given the unfavourable conditions they faced and the tilted balance of power that remained unassailably propitious to Israel. Those who opposed it argued that it simply constituted surrender to Israel, by recognizing the Israeli state and officially dropping the armed struggle without any concrete gains. In the five-year interim period there was to be no addressing any of the major Palestinian issues such the right of refugees to return, the status of Jerusalem, the control over Palestinian borders, and the dismantling of the Israeli settlements build intensively in the occupied West Bank and the Gaza Strip. According to the Accords, these issues were all to be relegated to the final talks, which as it turned out, would never take place anyway.

Hamas has consistently opposed the Oslo Agreement, believing that it was designed to serve Israeli interests and compromised basic Palestinian rights. After more than ten years of Oslo, the Palestinians had become completely frustrated and their initial shaky trust in the sincerity of peace talks with Israel had evaporated. During the interim period of years that would supposedly pave the way for permanent peace, Israel did everything possible to worsen the life of Palestinians and enhance its colonial occupation of the West Bank and Gaza Strip. During that period of time, for example, the size and number of Israeli colonial settlements in the West Bank – a major obstacle facing any final peace agreement – doubled. With the failure of Oslo, a second *intifada* erupted in 2000 against Israel, giving more power and influence to Hamas and its 'resistance project'.

In March 2005 Hamas made three successive historic decisions, each of which represents a milestone in the movement's political life. The movement decided to run for the Palestinian Legislative Council elections in the West Bank and Gaza Strip. It decided that along with other Palestinian factions it would put on hold all military activities, for an unspecified amount of time and on its own terms. And it considered joining the PLO.

Hamas seemed to have decided to move firmly towards the top of the Palestinian leadership. The most important of these three milestones was Hamas's decision to participate in the legislative elections in January 2006. This decision was completely in the opposite direction to its previous refusal to take part in 1996 elections because Hamas perceived them as an outcome of the Oslo Accords. By way of justification of the new move it put forward the new conditions since the September 2000 *intifada.* Hamas was also becoming confident of its own strength, after having won almost two-thirds of the seats in the January 2005 partial municipal elections.

Hamas's decision to take part in the elections had a profound impact on the nature of the movement, on the Palestinian political scene and on the peace process at large. At the level of its internal make-up, it would help politicize the movement – at the expense of its well-known militarism.

HAMAS

Founded in the late 1980s, Hamas emerged as a doubly driven religious-nationalist liberation movement which peacefully preaches the Islamic religious call while harmoniously embracing the strategy of armed struggle against an occupying Israel. Its critics thought it seemed as if Hamas started where the PLO had left off. Its supporters felt that Hamas came at just the right time to salvage the Palestinian national struggle from complete capitulation to Israel. On the ground, Hamas hacked its own path in almost the opposite direction to the peaceful route then being taken by the PLO and other Arab countries that had concluded peace treaties with Israel, namely Egypt and Jordan. It refused to come under the PLO as the wider umbrella of the Palestinian nationalist struggle, and adopted the 'old' call for the 'liberation of Palestine' as it had been originally enshrined by the PLO founders back in the mid-1960s. Hamas rejected the idea of concluding peace treaties with Israel that were conditional on full Palestinian recognition of the right of Israel to exist.

With the lack of any serious breakthrough toward achieving even a minimum level of Palestinian rights, Hamas has sustained a continuous rise since its inception. After years of persistent struggle it has become a key player both within the parameters of the Arab and Palestinian-Israeli conflict and in the arena of political Islam in the region. At the Palestinian level, it has shown a continuing popular appeal. By using myriad and interconnected strategies spanning military attacks, educational, social and charitable work in addition to religious propagation, it has succeeded in popularizing itself across the Palestinian constituencies inside and outside Palestine. With the gradual erosion of both the legitimacy and popularity of the PLO, Hamas's power has manifested itself in landslide victories in municipal elections, student union elections, syndicational and other elections held in the West Bank and the Gaza Strip.

In the area of political Islam and its various approaches to politics, Hamas has offered a unique contemporary case of an Islamist movement that is engaged in a liberation struggle against a foreign occupation. Islamist movements have been driven by a host of various causes, the vast majority of which were focused on the corrupt regimes of their own countries. Another stream of movements, the 'globalized Jihadists', have expanded their 'holy campaigns' across geopolitical lines, furthering pan-Islamic notions that reject ideas of individual Muslim nation-states. Contrary to both of these, Hamas has somehow remained nation-state based, limiting its struggle to one for and within Palestine, and fighting not a local regime but a foreign occupier. This differentiation is important as it exposes the shallowness of the widespread (mostly Western) trivializing conflation of all Islamist movements into one single 'terrorist' category.

Hamas has undergone various developments and experiences, and there are clear maturational differences between its early years and its later phases. Over the years of the struggle, at historic junctures and decisive and sensitive turning points, Hamas has offered not only a fascinating case for study but more importantly a case of an emerging key player capable of affecting the course and the outcome of the Palestinian-Israeli conflict.

Vacillating between its strong religious foundations and political nationalist agendas, Hamas strives to keep a balance between its ultimate vision and immediate pressing realties. Although it will remain an open question to what extent the 'religious' and the 'political' constitute the make-up of Hamas, it is significant to witness the interplay between these two drives within the movement. Although the movement suppresses any implicit or explicit tension between the two, it is perhaps only a question of time and space, and the nature of certain events, before one of them succeeds in overriding the other. At the highly politicized junctures of Hamas's life, it has been clearly evident that the 'political' vigorously occupies the driver's seat.

Militarily, Hamas adopted the controversial tactic of 'suicide bombing', to which its name has become attached in the West and the rest of the world. The first use of this tactic was in 1994, in retaliation for a massacre of Palestinians praying in a mosque in the Palestinian city of Hebron. A fanatical Jewish settler opened machine gun fire upon the worshippers, killing 29 and injuring many more. Hamas vowed to revenge these killings, and so it did. Since then all and each of Hamas's vicious attacks against Israeli civilians have been directly linked to specific Israeli atrocities against Palestinian civilians.

Although no more brutal than what the Israelis have been doing to Palestinians for decades, the suicide attacks have damaged the reputation of both Hamas and the Palestinians worldwide. Hamas's justification for conducting these kinds of operation has many grounds. First, it says that these operations are the exception to the rule and only driven by the need to retaliate. It is an 'eye for an eye' policy in response to the continual killing of Palestinian civilians by the Israeli army. Second, Hamas says that it keeps extending an offer to Israel by which civilians on both sides would be spared from being targeted, but Israel has never accepted this offer. Third, Hamas leaders say that Israeli society as a whole should pay the price of the occupation of the West Bank and Gaza Strip, just as much as Palestinian society is paying the price for that occupation: fear and suffering should be felt on both sides.

At the socio-cultural level, Hamas has had mixed fortunes. Its grassroots social work in helping the poor and supporting hundreds of thousands of Palestinians has been admired and praised. This sustained work, which has been marked by competence and dedicated sincerity, has bestowed on the movement a high level of popularity. At election times this has paid off considerably. Combined with its military and confrontational action against Israel, Hamas has been functioning on several fronts at the same time, and this has not failed to impress the Palestinians.

However, many secular Palestinians have feared that Hamas has been indirectly, if incrementally, transforming the cultural and social fabric of Palestinian society. Hamas has seemingly exploited its socio-political capital and popularity to advance its cultural and religious agenda. Although there have been only a few occasions when Hamas members have attempted to impose certain religious morals on society, and these cannot really be described as a phenomenon, they have been enough to create anxiety among more secular Palestinians. Many Palestinians support the nationalist/liberationalist and social work of Hamas, but not its religious ideal. Hamas purposefully overlooks this fact, and instead considers any vote for its political agenda as a vote for its religious one too.

HAMAS IN POWER

The reasons behind the Hamas victory in the 2006 Palestinian Legislative Council (PLC) elections, and the significance of this victory, merit a closer look. Hamas triumphed for a host of reasons. In the first place the movement has indeed reaped the benefits of long years of devoted work and popularity among the Palestinians. At least half the voters supported Hamas for its programme and its declared objectives; also for its warmth and the helping hands that it has kept close to the poor and needy. The other half of Hamas's voters was driven by other forces. The failure of the peace process, combined with the ever-increasing brutality of the Israeli occupation, left the Palestinians with no faith in the option of negotiating a peaceful settlement with Israel.

The gap in the debate on 'peace talks versus resistance' was closing as the date of the election approached, with the notion of 'peace talks' losing ground, yet without clear and definite support for Hamas's 'resistance' concept either. The latter was vague, and many Palestinians were wary about its meaning and mechanisms. But the frustration of the peace talks had by then taken its toll, and contributed largely to the defeat of the Fatah movement, the upholder and main force of the Oslo Agreements and what had resulted from them.

Another major factor that helped Hamas in winning those elections was the failure of the Fatah-led Palestinian Authority in almost in all aspects. It failed not only externally, on the front of the peace talks with Israel, but also internally, with its management of day-to-day services to the Palestinian people. Mismanagement, corruption and theft were the 'attributes' that came to mark Fatah's top leaders, ministers and high-ranking staff. As unemployment and poverty reached unprecedented levels, the extravagant lifestyle of senior Palestinian officials infuriated the public. The elections gave the people the chance to punish those officials. The chickens were coming home to roost, and Hamas was to be the beneficiary.

Thus, it can hardly be said that the Palestinian people voted for Hamas primarily on religious grounds. There was certainly no overnight popular conversion to Hamas's religious fervour or even its political ideology. Christians and secular people voted for Hamas side by side with Hamas members and exponents in all constituencies. Hamas's support of Christian candidates won them seats in the parliament. A Christian was appointed to the Hamas cabinet as the minister of tourism. The vast spectrum of Hamas's voters in these elections supported the suggestion that the people were voting for new blood, and for a nationalist liberation movement that promised change and reform on all fronts, more than for Hamas the religious group.

The Hamas election victory itself represents something significant not only for Palestinians but also for other Arabs, Muslims and beyond. At the Palestinian level it is a historic turning point, where a major shift has taken place in the leadership of the national liberation movement. For the first time in more than half a century Palestinian Islamists have moved into the driver's seat of the Palestinian national movement. It seems that almost overnight the Islamists have replaced the long-lived secular leadership that controlled the destiny of the Palestinians and their national decision making for decades. This fundamental change, furthermore, was realized through peaceful means and without violence, giving Palestinians as a whole – including Hamas – a great sense of pride. Not only are the Palestinians theoretically competent and ready to practise democratic rule, they have done so by embracing democracy on the ground and accepting its outcome. Moreover, the campaigns for the elections with their contrasting platforms gave the Palestinians the chance to revisit their strategy over the conflict with Israel, as it had previously been designed and pursued by the Fatah movement.

For Hamas itself, this victory is the greatest challenge that the movement has faced since its emergence. Almost abruptly, all Hamas's ideals and slogans have been brought down to earth to face the harsh realities on the ground. It could be safely said that the post-election Hamas will be considerably different from the organization we used to know before the elections. At the Arab and Muslim level, Hamas's victory is almost unique: political Islam has reached power in a democratic process and will not be deprived of its victory. Islamist movements throughout the region were jubilant at Hamas's triumph and considered it to be their own victory. Existing Arab and Muslim regimes, on the other hand, have watched the rise of Hamas to power with obvious anxiety and suspicion, and fear that it will encourage their local

Islamists to vigorously pursue power. Secular constituencies and individuals in the Arab countries remain divided. They support the nationalist liberation side of Hamas, but they continue to be agitated by its religious and social substance.

At the international level, a Palestinian government led by Hamas has been a most unwelcome phenomenon among the fruits of democracy. The West in particular is now caught in the dilemma of either accepting this disquieting result, to show the Arab and Muslim world that its call for democracy in the region is sincere, or joining Israeli efforts to bring down Hamas's government and risk losing credibility. The West decided early on to join the blockade on the new Hamas government, as part of a concerted effort by Israel, the United States, the European Union, some Arab states and the Fatah movement to oust it.

Strategically, many Palestinians have looked at Hamas's victory as benefiting the ultimate ends of the Palestinian national-ist movement in both the short and long term. Hamas's presence at the heart of the Palestinian decision-making mechanism furnishes further, and much needed, legitimacy to the Palestinian Authority. It also brings more integrity and trust to the entire make-up of Palestinian politics. Hamas had never previously participated in the Palestinian Authority constructed by the Oslo Accords, on the basis that both the Accords and the Authority had capitulated to Israel and made unacceptable concessions. Capitalizing on a 'free-ride' type of discourse, Hamas has not only succeeded in amassing astonishing popularity: it also challenged the leading position of Fatah, the backbone of the PLO and the strongest party in mainstream Palestinian society. The inclusion of Hamas in the political process will now deprive Fatah of the erstwhile free-ride politics it came to abuse, and ensure it is held responsible for more 'real' politics along with other Palestinian parties.

More importantly, and at the level of the conflict with

Israel, there cannot be a sustainable and final peace deal without a real Palestinian consensus, to which Hamas's contribution is central. Hamas's political position is pragmatic and hovers around accepting the concept of a two-state solution. If a decent final agreement can be reached, recognizing Palestinian rights according to Madrid Conference references and UN resolutions, Hamas will be unable to object. A moderate, co-opted and participating Hamas, even if it hardens the PA position, is far better than a radicalized and militarized Hamas.

1 Hamas's history

ISLAMISM AND THE PALESTINIAN STRUGGLE

How are Islam and Palestine interrelated?

Over the centuries, Islam and Palestine have been intimately linked in the imagery and history of Muslims. Palestine has been bestowed with Islamic holiness, as well as religious significance for Christian and Jewish people, for a host of reasons and historic events. Jerusalem, and in particular *al-Masjid al-Aqsa* (the furthest mosque), is the first place to which Muslims directed their prayers when the Prophet Muhammad started preaching Islam in Arabia in the early seventh century. *Bait al-Maqdes*, or Jerusalem, is the third holiest place in Islam after Mecca and Medina in Arabia. It is frequently referred to in the *Quran*, and is given numerous mentions in the sayings – *Hadith* – of the Prophets. Most of the stories about God's messengers as related in the *Quran* have specific geographical references to Palestine. One full chapter in the *Quran, sourat al-Isra,* is dedicated to the Prophet Muhammad's journey from Mecca to Jerusalem, and his ascension there to heaven to meet God. This is a chapter passionately embraced by Muslims the world over as one of the most astonishing divine stories. On the very rock where the Prophet set off on his journey to heaven, the Dome of the Rock was built, adjacent to the spot where the Jews say the Old Temple of Solomon was built.

The Christian and Jewish religious significance of Palestine is also recognized in Islam. Jesus Christ, who was born in Palestine, and Moses, who migrated to it, are considered by the *Quran* and Muslims to be two of the five most highly regarded prophets of God (the other three being Muhammad, Ibrahim and Ismail).

Added to its religious sacredness, Palestine has long occupied a geo-strategic position, linking the African and Asian parts of the Middle East, offering a long coast and rich passage on the Mediterranean between the Arabian peninsula, Egypt and Greater Syria. Because of its religious and strategic significance Palestine was destined to be the field of wars and invasions. Muslims conquered Palestine and brought it under their control in 638 AD. Since then Islam has been a central feature of the political, cultural and emotional foundation of this ancient tract of land.

The Western Crusaders from 1097 onward for 200 years fought war after war to gain control over Palestine, and in particular Jerusalem, and bring it within Christendom. The Muslims, who at that point already had ruled Palestine for over 400 years, had long allowed people of other religions to live in peace in their lands. Muslims had long welcomed pilgrims of all religions, and had made accessible all of the historical shrines of religious significance to themselves and others: Christians, Jews, Persians, Orthodox Christians, Coptics and many others. Palestine was part of an ancient area, sacred to many people.

After 400 years of open exchange, and to the humiliation of Muslims, the Crusaders ruthlessly took Jerusalem, slaughtered its Muslim inhabitants and succeeded in ruling there for 70 years. When Saladin defeated the Crusaders in 1187 AD he entered the imagination and history of Islam as one of its most prominent heroes, whose successes signified the end of Muslim disgrace and defeat. The name of Saladin brings to Muslims and Palestinians memories of glory, and for many of them it emphasizes the inevitable will and capacity to rise from the ashes. Perceived as brutal foreign invasions launched by European Christians, the Crusades are still seen by many Arabs and Palestinians as the original blueprint for the Zionist invasion, which also had it roots in Europe.

What is the relationship between Islam and Palestine within the Arab-Israeli conflict?

In the consciousness of many Muslims, the identity of the ruler of Palestine indicates the strength or weakness of Islam and Muslims. If Palestine is ruled and controlled by foreigners and non-Muslims – from the Crusaders of the medieval ages to the Zionists of the twentieth century and the present – then Islam and Muslims perceive themselves to be weak and defeated.

After the final defeat of the Crusaders in 1291, Palestine remained under Muslim rule for over 700 additional years, until the break-up of the Muslim Ottoman Empire which had ruled Palestine, in the aftermath of World War I. The collapse of this declining Turkish empire, which had sided with the German allies in the Great War, was met with scant specific regret and loyalty by many in Palestine and the rest of the Arab world, because of the recent brutality of its reign. However the Ottoman foundation in Islam had kept Palestine firmly fixed within the Arab and Muslim world.

With the complete political collapse of the Empire in the wake of the armistice, Ottoman territories in the Middle East were carved up into temporary protectorates controlled by the European victors, until more permanent political configurations could be concluded. Palestine fell under British colonial control between 1917 and 1948. While the centuries-long roots of Islamic heritage and allegiance in Palestine were self-evident, strong currents of

Zionism had long infiltrated British thinking. As early as 1917 Balfour had expressed his intention to support a Jewish national homeland in Palestine, and with the surge of Jewish refugees fleeing increasingly larger Nazi-controlled parts of Europe, Jewish immigration into British-administered Palestine escalated between the 1920s and 1940s.

Fighting what were clearly perceived to be colonial powers, Arab liberation movements across the former Ottoman territories united across their assorted versions of Islam and individual nationalism, and attempted to maximize the mobilization capacities of both tenets. In Palestine, Palestinians revolted against the British mandate during the 1920s to 1940s under just such a blended Islamic banner.

But the fate of Palestine would be irrevocably compounded by factors beyond the simple struggle between colonizers and colonized. By 1948 Britain's control over Palestine was severely compromised by its own state of economic depletion following World War II, and ironically, by the relentless intensity of Zionist terrorist attacks. With mounting international sympathy for Jewish settlement in Palestine, the United Nations proposed a partitioning scheme in 1947 giving the mostly immigrant 600,000 Jews in Palestine the coastal and rich 54 per cent of the land, leaving the remaining part for the 1.4 million Palestinians. At the time of the partion scheme, Jewish ownership of the land was merely 5.5 per cent. In May 1948, a depleted Britain withdrew from a Palestine already descending into Arab/Jewish war. A Jewish state of Israel was declared almost immediately on 15 May, and was recognized instantly by the United States. Palestinians had been dumped into an abyss of chaos in their own land.

One of the most popular rebellion movements against the British, often recalled with pride by Palestinians, is the Izzedin al-Qassam movement of the 1930s. Sheikh Izzedin al-Qassam was a religious scholar who launched a *Jihad* against the colonial British and their allies, the increasingly militarized European Zionist settlers who by then were flooding Palestine. Decades on, in the early 1990s Hamas's military wing would be named after Sheikh al-Qassam.

When the Zionist intentions became evident of creating a Jewish homeland in Palestine, with the strong support of the European powers, Palestinians tried as early as the beginning of the 1920s to mobilize their Muslim brethren the world over to defend Jerusalem and its holy places. In the year 1931, the first Islamic conference to defend *Bait al-Maqdes* was convened in Jerusalem, with delegations from Muslim countries as far distant as Iran, Tunisia and Pakistan. Muslim organisations and activities intensified in Palestine in parallel with the increase of activities and the militarization of the Zionist organizations and their settlers.

With the creation of Israel in 1948, a wide shock of humiliation reverberated across the Muslim world. The Jews occupied more than two-thirds of Palestine and Jerusalem, and were but a few steps from the al-Aqsa Mosque. The Arabs had been outmanoeuvred by Zionist might and its British collusion. This defeat was astounding, and the disgrace cut deeply into the psyche of Palestinians, Arabs and Muslims. Since then, Islam has at times been called upon as an indigenous ideology entrenched throughout Muslim society, which could be used as a rallying point of mobilization in the battle against the enemy and its state as erected in Palestine.

In the 1950s and 1960s Arabs and Palestinians were strongly influenced by nationalist and Marxist ideologies in their campaign to fight Israel and liberate Palestine. As a result, in Palestine and the surrounding countries bordering Israel – Egypt, Syria and Jordan – as well as in more distant countries such as Iraq, Libya and Algeria, Islamist tendencies were sidelined and Islam as an ideology of mobilization was relegated to the back seat.

Another, and even more mortifying, defeat was looming for the Palestinians and the Arabs in 1967, when Israel launched devastating attacks on Egypt, Syria and Jordan, annexing more land from all of them: Sinai and the Gaza Strip from Egypt, the Golan Heights from Syria and the West Bank with East Jerusalem and the al-Aqsa Mosque from Jordan. With this collapse of the Arab armies, nationalist and Marxist ideologies started to give way to the gradual rise of Islamist movements and political Islam. Starting from the mid-1970s Palestinian Islamists, in the current usage of the word, started establishing stronger footholds in Palestinian cities. With the victory of the Iranian revolution in the late 1970s, and the defeat of the PLO in Lebanon in 1982, the Palestinian Islamists were steadily on the rise. Their main nationalist rival, the National Movement for the Liberation of Palestine (Fatah), had started its long decline. Islam was once again being recalled to the heart of Palestinian politics.

THE MUSLIM BROTHERHOOD ROOTS OF HAMAS

Who are the Muslim Brothers?

In its original thinking and make-up, Hamas belongs to the realm of Muslim Brotherhood movements in the region. These were first established in Egypt in 1928 on the eve of the collapse of the Ottoman Empire. As the major Islamist movement, the Muslim Brotherhood could be considered to be the 'mother of all movements that comprise political Islam' in the Middle East (with the exception of Iran). Over the past eight decades, its branches have been established in almost every

Arab country, and beyond, blending religion and politics to the greatest degree. The Palestinian branch was set up in Jerusalem in 1946, two years before the establishment of the state of Israel.

Although the Muslim Brotherhood was initially main-stream and relatively moderate, many radical small groups have sprouted from it over decades. The influence of its main thinkers, mainly Sayyed Qutob, has had an enormous impact on various strands of political Islam the world over. The main objective of the individual Muslim Brotherhood movements is to establish Islamic states in each of their countries, with the ultimate utopia of uniting individual Islamic states into one single state representing the *Ummah*, or Muslim nation.

The Muslim Brotherhood movements, and movements that share the same intellectual background and understanding, are presently the most powerful and active political movements in the Middle East. Robustly represented on the political scene, its members enjoy parliamentary legitimacy or government posts in countries such as Egypt, Jordan, Yemen, Kuwait, Morocco, Sudan, Algeria, Iraq and Bahrain. They are also strongly repre-sented in the outlawed opposition in places such as Libya, Tunisia, Syria and Saudi Arabia. Although they share the same background and sources of teaching, these movements are greatly coloured by their own nationalist concerns and agenda. There is no obligatory hierarchical organizational structure that combines all of them into one single transnational organization.

Islamist movements, historically and currently, differ greatly in their understanding and interpretation of Islam. In any discussion of the Hamas movement, the two major issues that need to be distinguished are the differing perceptions of various Islamist movements concerning the 'ends' versus the 'means'. The 'ends' issue denotes the extent to which politics is ingrained in Islam, whereas the 'means' issue reflects the controversy on the use of violence to achieve the 'ends'. The spectrum of such interpretations tends to vacillate between two extremes. At one end there is an understanding of Islam that politicizes religion and renders it the ultimate judge in all aspects of life, including politics. At the other end, there is a different interpretation and an apolitical understanding of Islam, where it is argued that efforts should be focused on morals and religious teachings, away from politics and state-making, and where the sole accepted ways of conveying the word of Islam are peaceful ones.

Along the spectrum of Islamist movements, the Muslim Brotherhood occupies almost the centre of the continuum in terms of 'ends' and 'means'. The Muslim Brotherhood believes in politicized religion and religious politics, hence its strong conviction that Islamic states must be established. It became established that the means to realize this end were undoubtedly peaceful, as had been stressed by the movement's founders back in the Egypt of the 1930s. Yet over the following decades, groups within the Muslim Brotherhood adopted violence and clashed with governments in Egypt and Syria. Since the mid-1980s they have overwhelmingly adhered to peaceful means, even when confronted with extreme oppressive measures, as was the case with the Tunisian Islamist movement in the late 1980s and afterwards.

On one side of the Muslim Brotherhood's centre position on this ends/means continuum, there are groups such as al-Qaeda which embrace violence wholeheartedly in their pursuit of their political aims. Hamas also lies somewhere on this side of the continuum, but closer to the Muslim Brotherhood than to al-Qaeda, by virtue of its unique specificity of using violence only against foreign occupying powers and not against national governments. On the other side of the Muslim Brotherhood there are smaller groups that distance themselves from politics, such as al-Dawa wal Tabligh, which believes only in spreading religious teaching and morality, and Hizb al-Tahrir, whose politicization of religion is perhaps stronger than that of the Muslim Brotherhood, but it believes neither in violence nor in political participation in existing systems. For it, the fight is purely intellectual.

What are the links between the Muslim Brotherhood, Palestine and Hamas?

Hamas represents the internal metamorphosis of the Palestinian Muslim Brotherhoods which took place in the late 1980s. Officially, the Palestinian branch of the Muslim Brotherhood was founded in 1946 in Jerusalem, although its presence and activities in Palestine go back to 1943/4 in Gaza City, Jerusalem, Nablus and other cities. The aims, structure and outlook of the Palestinian Muslim Brotherhood were drawn along the main lines of thinking of the mother organization in Egypt, where Islamization of society is the prime goal. At this time there was no Israel, and Islamists were dealing with the British mandate and the growing power of the Zionist movement.

There is no strong record of the Palestinian Muslim Brotherhood fighting against British troops in Palestine during the mandate period. The Egyptian Muslim Brotherhood, however, took part in the 1948 war against the British by sending hundreds of volunteers to fight alongside the then-weak Egyptian army. After the creation of the state of Israel in 1948, the Palestinian Muslim Brotherhood was physically divided into two parts; one in the West Bank which was annexed to Jordan and where the Palestinian Muslim Brotherhood joined the Jordanian Branch of the Muslim Brotherhood, and one in the Gaza Strip, which was left under Egyptian administration, and thus the Palestinian Muslim Brotherhood there became close to the Egyptian Muslim Brotherhood.

By the war of 1967, new political and geographical realities were brought into being when the entire area of historic Palestine, including the West Bank and the Gaza Strip, fell under Israeli control. The two wings of the Palestinian Muslim Brotherhood, the Gazan and the West Bank, became closer and developed unitary structures over the years. In the 1970s and 1980s, the Palestinian Muslim Brotherhood amassed strength and established footholds in all major Palestinian cities. On the broader Palestinian political scene, leftist and nationalist movements had been outpacing and outpowering the Muslim Brotherhood in both Gaza and the West Bank from as early as the 1940s up to the late 1980s. In particular, the Fatah movement (the Palestinian National Liberation Movement), and the PLO (the Palestine Liberation Organization) which is the wider umbrella of the national Palestinian movements, dominated Palestinian politics over those decades.

The 1980s witnessed a rapid growth in the power of the Muslim Brotherhood. In December 1987 a popular Palestinian uprising, the *intifada*, against the Israeli occupation erupted first in the Gaza Strip, then in the West Bank. On the eve of that uprising, the Palestinian Muslim Brotherhood decided to undertake a major transformation within the movement. It established Hamas as an adjunct organisation with the specific mission of confronting the Israeli occupation.

Are there other Islamist movements in Palestine?

There have been, and still are, Islamist movements other than Hamas in Palestine. The most important one is the Islamic Jihad Movement, established in early 1980s, at least five years before the emergence of Hamas. The Islamic Jihad was formed by discontented former members of both the Muslim Brother-hoods, Fatah and other nationalist and leftist Palestinian factions. Inspired by the victory of the Islamic revolution in Iran in 1978/9, the idea of the Islamic Jihad was to form a bridge between Islam and Palestine, which were separately represented by the Muslim Brotherhood on the one hand, and the nationalist camp (the PLO) on the other hand.

When the Palestinian Muslim Brotherhood (MB), the mother organization of Hamas, was immersed in its religious programmes in the first years of 1980s, the Islamic Jihad offered a new version of nationalist Islam which incorpo-rated the struggle against Israel into the very heart of Islamic discourse and practice. Between 1982 and 1987, the Islamic Jihad posed a serious challenge to the Muslim Brotherhood because of its adoption of military resistance against the Israeli occupation. It also posed an equal challenge to the nationalist factions whose main criticism of the Muslim Brotherhood concerned its deferment of confrontation with the occupation. If the PLO was nationalist enough, but lacked an Islamic dimension, and if the Palestinian MB was Islamist enough, but lacked a nationalist dimension, the Islamic Jihad combined both components and had ended what it had seen to be a disconnection between Islam and Palestine.

In the second half of the 1990s, and during the second Palestinian uprising in the year 2000, the Islamic Jihad carried out many suicide attacks. At certain periods, it outpaced Hamas and other factions in this practice. However, the Islamic Jihad is weak in its membership and networking, and this is why it shows little enthusiasm for elections. Its justification is that elections absorb national energy that should be directed toward resisting the Israelis. In the 1990s whenever the Islamic Jihad took part in even minor elections for student unions or trade unions, its results ranged between 4 and 7 per cent compared with 45 to 55 per cent for Hamas.

Another Islamist movement with a certain visible presence in Palestine, if with less current relevance, is Hizb al-Tahrir (the Liberation Party). It was founded in 1952 as a splinter group of the Muslim Brotherhood. Its main belief is that the source of all sins in Muslim societies is the disappearance of Khilafa, the overarching Muslim rule, and that all efforts should be focused on restoring Khilafa. Once in power, the Khalifa (the person representing the supreme Islamic authority) can mobilize Muslims by virtue of his appeal, and his power if necessary, and direct them to work for any cause. The failure of Muslims (including Palestinians), Hizb al-Tahrir concludes, stems from their overlooking this premise. Grassroots efforts and gradual Islamization are fruitless. Change should be undertaken from above, and when the Khalifa is in power, many problems that face Muslims will be solved. Regarding the Palestinian question and confronting the Israeli occupation, Hizb al-Tahrir maintains a passive approach which has lost it popularity and leverage among Palestinians. The party opposes all forms of political participation, such as elections, and, in the absence of the Khalifa, it opposes a resort to violence against either national governments or Israel.

THE FORMATION OF HAMAS

When, why and how was Hamas founded?

Hamas came into being officially on 14 December 1987, declaring itself in an official communiqué a few days after the eruption of the first *intifada*, the Palestinian uprising, on 8 December. The decision to establish the Islamic Resistance

Movement (Hamas) was taken on the day following the *intifada* by top leaders of the Palestinian Muslim Brothers, Sheikh Ahmad Yassin, Abdul 'Aziz al-Rantisi, Salah Shehadeh, Muhammad sham'ah, 'Isa al-Nashar, 'Abdul Fattah Dukhan and Ibrahim al-Yazuri. (The first three were assassinated by Israel in later years.)

Hamas was formed by the Palestinian Muslim Brotherhood itself in order to respond to a number of factors pressing upon the organization. Internally and by the time of the *intifada*, the rank and file of the Palestinian Muslim Brotherhood were witnessing intense internal debate on the passive approach to the Israeli occupation. There were two opposing views. One pushed for a change in policy toward confrontation with the occupation, thus bypassing old and traditional thinking whose focus was on the Islamization of society first. The other view clung to the classical school of thought within the Muslim Brotherhood movements, which adhered to the concept of 'preparing the generations for a battle' which had no deadline. When the *intifada* erupted, the exponents of the confrontational policy gained a stronger position, arguing that Islamists would suffer a great loss if they decided not to take part in the *intifada*, definitively and equally with all the other participating Palestinian factions.

Externally, hard living conditions for Palestinians in the Gaza Strip, which had been created and exacerbated by the Israeli occupation, reached an unprecedented state. Poverty combined with feelings of oppression and humiliation charged the Palestinian atmosphere with the ripe conditions for revolt against the occupation. The *intifada* was the flashpoint. The explosion reflected the accumulation of past experiences and suffering more than any specific event that triggered things on the first day of the uprising. Strategically speaking, it was the golden opportunity for the Palestinian

Muslim Brotherhood to heed (and be seen to lead) the uprising. It did just so by creating Hamas.

Externally there was the factor of the rivalry at this time from a similar Islamic organization, not as national or leftist as the Islamic Jihad. As discussed above, the Islamic Jihad Movement had been on the rise during the few years preceding the *intifada*. The very incident that triggered the *intifada* itself involved Islamic Jihad members who freed themselves from an Israeli prison and engaged in a shoot-out with the Israeli soldiers. Feeling envious of the Islamic Jihad and its members, who emerged as heroes in the eyes of the Palestinians after the incident, the Palestinian Muslim Brotherhood felt the danger of losing ground to its small, yet more active, competitor. The presence and activities of the Islamic Jihad partly compelled the Muslim Brotherhood to speed up its internal transformation.

Why did the Palestinian Islamists only start their armed struggle against Israeli occupation in 1987 when this occupation started in 1967?

In the thinking of the Muslim Brothers, both in Palestine prior to the creation of Hamas and in other countries, the failures of Muslims – their backwardness, weakness and their defeat by their enemies – were the results of their deviation from the true path of Islam. Therefore, the proper process for redressing all of these failures, including the defeat in the wars against Israel, was first to educate Muslims about Islam and make them committed to their religion. Transforming people from ignorant Muslims into adherents would rehabilitate all of Muslim society and prepare it for the fight with its enemies, from the certainty of standing on strong ground. In the rhetoric of the Muslim Brotherhood this was called 'preparing the generations'.

The Palestinian Muslim Brothers had a deep conviction in

this principle, which they consistently used to justify their non-confrontation policy against the Israeli occupation during the 1950s, 1960s, 1970s and until 1987. Against mounting accusations by other Palestinian nationalist and leftist organisations of cowardice or even of being indirectly in the service of the Israeli occupation, the Palestinian Islamists clung to their strategy of 'preparing the generations' for a long time. They argued that it was a fruitless effort to fight Israel with a 'corrupt army'; instead one should build a devoted and religiously committed army, then engage in war against Israel.

This strategy came under continuous attack. For Palestinian nationalists and leftists, such an approach was a mere justification for refraining from joining the national struggle. It was also criticized as naive on two levels, the first being the association of an individual's capacity and genuine intention to fight the occupation with his or her level of religious commitment, and the second being the contrast between the open-ended abstraction of 'preparing the generations' with the daily imperative of engagement with the enemy. The true preparation of people to fight for their national rights and liberation, critics argued, is to fully engage in the struggle, where people learn and empower themselves as they advance and suffer. Moreover, Israel was understandably happy with the Islamists' concept of 'delaying the struggle' until the Palestinian generations were spiritually and morally well prepared and ready.

Hamas's supporters retrospectively defend the earlier thinking of their mother organization. They say that it was just exactly this strategy that guaranteed a strong beginning for Hamas and its continuous achievements on the ground in the years which followed. For them, the need for gradual and patient preparation was actually justified because in the 1960s and 1970s the Islamists were militarily very weak, and had they involved themselves in fruitless confrontation against Israel then, they would have been crushed easily, serving neither Palestine nor Islam.

Regardless of their rationalizations, the Islamists paid a high price during the decades when they opted for a non-confrontational policy. They provided the opportunity for their national rivals to outpace them, and put themselves in a disadvantageous position. More importantly, they deprived the Palestinian struggle against the Israeli occupation of the participation and contribution of that significant segment of the Palestinian population who came under the influence of the Palestinian Muslim Brotherhood and its thinking.

2 Hamas's ideology, strategy and objectives

THE DEFINITION OF HAMAS, ITS IDEOLOGICAL DRIVE AND WORLDVIEW

What is Hamas, and is it driven by religious or political convictions?

Perhaps the most informative answer to this common question can be found in a lengthy self-definition that Hamas once produced by way of introducing itself to a European government, years prior to its assuming power in 2006. In this self-definition, Hamas states its aims and strategies in addition to its long-term view for the solution in Palestine. Hamas describes itself as follows:

> The Islamic Resistance Movement (Hamas) is a Palestinian national liberation movement that struggles for the liberation of the Palestinian occupied territories and for the recognition of the legitimate rights of Palestinians. Although it came into existence soon after the eruption of the first Palestinian intifadah (uprising) in December 1987 as an expression of the Palestinian people's anger against the continuation of the Israeli occupation of Palestinian land and persecution of the Palestinian people, Hamas' roots extend much deeper in history.

The movement's motivation for resistance has been expressed by its founder and leader Sheikh Ahmad Yassin: 'The movement struggles against Israel because it is the aggressing, usurping and oppressing state that day and night hoists the rifle in the face of our sons and daughters.'

Hamas considers itself to be an extension of an old tradition that goes back to the early twentieth century struggle against British and Zionist colonialism in Palestine. The fundamentals from which it derives its legitimacy are mirrored in the very name it chose for itself. Hamas, in the Islamic language, means that it derives its guiding principles from the doctrines and values of Islam. Islam is completely Hamas' ideological frame of reference. It is from the values of Islam that the movement seeks its inspiration in its mobilisation effort, and particularly in seeking to address the huge difference in material resources between the Palestinian people and their supporters on the one hand and Israel and its supporters on the other. ...

The forms of resistance adopted by Hamas stem from the same justifications upon which the national Palestinian resistance movement has based its struggle for more than a quarter of a century. At least the first ten articles of the Palestinian National Charter issued by the PLO show complete compatibility with Hamas' discourse as elaborated in its Charter and other declarations. Furthermore, the same justifications for resistance had, prior to the emergence of Hamas in December 1987, been recognised, or endorsed, by a variety of regional and international bodies such as the Arab League, the Islamic Conference Organisation, the Non-Aligned Movement and the United Nations. It is clearly recognised that the Israeli occupation of the West Bank and Gaza in 1967 is illegal in UN Security Council Resolutions 242 and 338. ...

In spite of the overwhelming militant image it has in the minds of many people in the West, Hamas is not a mere military faction. It is a political, cultural and social grass roots organisation that has a separate military wing specialising in armed resistance against Israeli occupation. Apart from this strategically secretive military wing, all other sections within Hamas function through overt public platforms. The military wing has its own leadership and recruiting mechanism.

Hamas's social and educational activities in the Occupied Territories have become so interwoven within the Palestinian community that neither the Israelis nor their peace partners in the Palestinian Authority have been able to extricate them one from the other. The fact of the matter is that Hamas, contrary to Israeli assessment, acts as an infrastructure to the numerous cultural, educational and social institutions in Gaza and the West Bank that render invaluable and irreplaceable services to the public. In other words, it is Hamas that gives life to these institutions and not the reverse. The Israelis have repeatedly told the PA to close them down. The PA has tried but failed. A crackdown on these institutions amounts to a declaration of war not against Hamas but against the Palestinian community as a whole.

It must be pointed out that the above text identifies Hamas with the Palestinians' struggle to liberate their land only. There is no implication, either explicit or tacit, of any intention to establish an Islamic state in Palestine in the future, or any similar goals advocated by other Islamist organizations. There is further discussion of this below.

What is Hamas's ultimate aim? Is it to establish an Islamic state in Palestine?

The vague idea of establishing an Islamic state in Palestine as mentioned in the early statements of the movement was quickly sidelined and surpassed. Even when it was repeated by members of Hamas it never amounted to any really serious proposal with thoughtfully considered details. If anything, its early reluctant existence, followed by almost complete disappearance in Hamas's documentation and discourse, reflected the tension in the minds of Hamas's leaders between the political and the religious. On one hand there is the subconscious urge to remain sincere to the pure pre-Hamas religious utopia where the dream of an Islamic state sought to fulfil the goals of the long-distant future. On the other hand, the oversimplification and naivety of this dream exposed the extent to which Hamas needed to become aware of the realities of what the Palestinians were dealing with, on the ground, day after day. In this light, the Hamas dream of a pure Islamic state was practically embarrassing, but the realization of this developed a more sophisticated Hamas, a Hamas content to look towards the actual needs of a Palestinian people under siege.

Palestinians across the spectrum of political convictions have struggled desperately for more than eight decades to extract even minimal legitimate rights, first from British occupiers following the 1922 Mandate, in which Britain was apportioned control of the part of the former Ottoman Empire that included Palestine, and then from 1948, when Britain withdrew from Palestine, leaving the Zionist organization to declare the Jewish state of Israel. Israel has essentially been occupying and colonizing not only those parts of Palestine 'allocated' to it by the UN 1947 division plan, but even large areas of Palestine that were not. After all these decades of struggle, the maximum that the Palestinian leadership has struggled to achieve, without success, has been the retention or recovery of no more than one-eighth of the historic land of Palestine.

The Islamic state put forth in early in Hamas literature was visualized to include the whole of Palestine from the River Jordan to the Mediterranean Sea. The question became, would Hamas wait in hope for full liberation of all historic Palestine, or would it seek to impose a temporary Islamic state in just the West Bank and the Gaza Strip if they were ever returned to the Palestinians? What kind of state would this be, and how would it deal with its surroundings, with Israel, with the world? On what basis would it do so? And so forth. There was a list of endless intractable questions surrounded this idea of establishing an Islamic state, and eventually it ended in complete trivialization, with Hamas dropping the idea altogether.

If not the formation of an Islamic state, then what now is Hamas's ultimate goal? A plain answer, suggested by the movement's formal declarations, is the total liberation of the historic land of Palestine from the River Jordan to the Mediterranean Sea. However, similar to the utopian religious goal of establishing an Islamic state, this utopian nationalist goal tends to be mentioned less and less in Hamas's documents and verbal statements. In fact, the longer Hamas functions, the less interest it shows in adopting or declaring 'ultimate goals'. Hamas has developed, and is still developing, into a movement that is more and more preoccupied with current and immediate, and medium-term, goals.

In the course of taking power after the elections of 2006, Hamas has focused its pre and post-elections discourse on the concept of explicitly resisting the Israeli occupation while implicitly if reluctantly accepting the principle of a two-state solution. Neither an Islamic state nor the total liberation of Palestine have been emphasized. The ultimate goals, thus, have been replaced with short and medium-term ones, more pressing and more realistic.

What is Hamas's strategy?

To confirm its move out of the realm of far-fetched dreams, Hamas started to advocate more achievable goals in both the short and medium term. It not only sought immediate relief and benefits for Palestinians on the ground now, it pursued goals that could be comprehended by regional and international audiences. Minimizing the religious in its use of language, Hamas's discourse has became more aware, embracing legal jargon and basing itself on the norms of international law. Yet Hamas still struggles to keep alive the principle of the 'liberation of Palestine' as a whole, in the mildest way possible, within the context of the immediate challenges faced by the movement and Palestinians at large. In the few years after the first *intifada* Hamas developed its strategy considerably from the initial raw statements mentioned in its charter. In 1993 it issued an 'Introductory Memorandum'. Under the heading 'The Movement's Strategy', it read:

> Hamas constructs its strategy for confronting the Zionist occupation as follows:
> - The Palestinian people, being the primary target of the occupation, bear the larger part of the burden in resisting it. Hamas, therefore, works to mobilize the energies of these people and to direct them toward steadfastness.

- The field of engagement with the enemy is Palestine, Arab and Islamic lands being fields of aid and support to our people, especially those lands that have been enriched with the pure blood of [Islamic] martyrs throughout the ages.
- Confronting and resisting the enemy in Palestine must be continuous until victory and liberation. Holy struggle in the name of God as our guide, and fighting and inflicting harm on enemy troops and their instruments rank at the top of our means of resistance.
- Political activity, in our view, is one means of holy struggle against the Zionist enemy and aims to buttress the struggle and steadfastness of our people and to mobilize its energies and that of our Arab Islamic nation to render our cause victorious.

In this strategy Hamas confirms the 'boundaries' of the armed conflict, stating clearly that it wishes to undertake no military steps outside Palestine: 'the field of engagement with the enemy is Palestine'. Hamas reiterates this conviction in its strategy to assure the outside world that attacking any western or even Israeli targets outside Palestine is not on the agenda of the movement.

It is worth mentioning that these guidelines were outlined 13 years before Hamas came to power and took control of the Palestinian Authority in January 2006. These broad proclamations of Hamas's strategy were drawn with very little expectation, if any, of where political and military developments concerning the Israeli-Palestinian conflict would lead the Palestinians. Surely it was beyond the imagination of the people who drafted the above strategy that Hamas would one day be allowed to win free and fair democratic elections to control a limited self-rule authority created according to peace agreements between Hamas's rivals and Israel.

This new situation has brought the cornerstone of Hamas's strategy – 'military resistance' to the Israeli occupation – under close scrutiny. In taking over a government of besieged and weakened authority, Hamas was overwhelmed by the numerous issues relating to the daily living of Palestinians. Any thought of military resistance appeared for a while to be a luxury that the movement could not afford. As was noted above, Hamas had pragmatically recognized earlier that the immediate welfare of the besieged Palestinian people was as important as any more long-term ideological ideals. It has managed to save face as the party of resistance by adopting the standard line that 'political activity ... is itself one of the means of struggle', a line echoed in the statement often made by its leaders that military resistance is not an end in itself, but a means to an end. Thus, being consumed in government undertakings and serving the Palestinian people on a daily basis can easily be linked to the broad parameters of resistance.

How does Hamas perceive the world?

Hamas's immediate world, as explained in its literature, comprises three concentric circles: the Palestinian core, the larger Arabic circle and the larger still embracing Islamic circle. Beyond those circles lies the rest of the world. The question of Palestine is, for Hamas, the fundamental determinant in shaping the relationship between those three circles and the rest of the world. The movement's literature states that:

> Hamas believes that the ongoing conflict between Arabs and Muslims and Zionists in Palestine is a fateful civilisational struggle incapable of being brought

to an end without eliminating its cause, namely, the Zionist settlement of Palestine.

The West is charged not only with the responsibility of having illegally created Israel but also with bringing devastation and dismemberment to the region as a whole:

> This enterprise of aggression [on Palestine] comple-ments the larger Western project that seeks to strip this Arab Islamic nation of its cultural roots in order to consolidate Western Zionist hegemony over it by completing the plan of greater Israel and establishing political and economic control of it. Doing so implies maintaining the [current] state of [physical] division, backwardness, and dependency in which this Arab Islamic nation is forced to live. The conflict as described is a form of struggle between truth and false-hood, which obligates Arabs and Muslims to support the Palestinians in bearing the consequences of a holy struggle to extirpate the Zionist presence from Pales-tine and prevent it from spreading to other Arab and Islamic countries.

Of the circles surrounding Palestine, the first one is Arabic, the second is Islamic and the third is the rest of the world. Naturally more affinity and intimacy is felt towards the closer Arabic and Islamic circles. There is a considerable amount of dismay, crit-icism and attack against the indifference that the outermost circle comprising the 'world' has exhibited concerning the suffering of the Palestinians. The western world is typically criticized and accused not only of 'transplanting' Israel in Palestine – at the heart of the Arab region – by force, but also with its continuous support of the 'usurping and aggressive

Zionist state' which has sought even to exceed the borders of the original illegal foundation.

In its very early stages, Hamas thinking was skewed by a dichotomy that bisected the world into the 'truthfulness' represented by Muslims and believers, and the 'falsehood' represented by non-Muslims and particularly westerners and Jews. This naïve perception later almost disappeared from the movement's discourses. In tandem with Hamas's rise in influence, the expansion of its regional and international relations and its realization of the complexity of reality and politics at ground level, Hamas has rehabilitated its 'worldview' and effectively abandoned the dichotomy based on believers/nonbelievers. The notion of political support for the Palestinians and their just cause has prevailed as the defining parameter by which Hamas assesses world players and where they stand.

HAMAS: A NATIONAL LIBERATION MOVEMENT OR A RELIGIOUS MOVEMENT?

What are the nationalist elements and religious elements in Hamas's thinking and practice?

Hamas is a blend of national liberation movement and Islamist religious group. By virtue of such a nature its driving forces are dual, its daily functioning is biaxial and its end goals are bifocal, where each side of each binary serves the other.

The dual driving reasons for Palestinians to join Hamas are to actively engage in the 'liberation of Palestine' by resisting the Israeli occupation and whatever else that may take, *and* to serve Islam and spread its word. The word 'and' is pivotal here and cannot be replaced by the word 'or', though the balance between the two motives need not be equal or the same in everyone. Hamas considers that its power is to be found in this link, the strengthened alloy of these two separate strands of Palestinian political activism: the national secular liberation movement that has confronted Israel, *and* the Islamist religious movement that largely has not. The desired thinking is that in struggling for the liberation of Palestine, an individual is serving Islam, and in strengthening the call of Islam this individual serves the liberation struggle.

In fact, this is one of the major underlying reasons explaining the continuous rise of Hamas. People with strong nationalist feelings and the drive to struggle against Israel, and with a traditional Islamist background, tend to choose Hamas as their natural movement. Others, with strong religious sentiments and who also want to be active against Israel, also join Hamas. Indeed, it is to be expected that both driving forces will occupy the mind and soul of the Hamas membership, but certainly their strengths differ at the level of individuals. For example, members of the Muslim Brotherhood organization who became de facto members of Hamas when the former was transformed into the latter tend to nurture a stronger religious drive than those members who joined Hamas in later stages and defected from other nationalist factions.

The day-to-day operations of Hamas are therefore spread along the axis of religious and nationalist activities. It devotes considerable efforts to educating its membership according to Islamic ideals, as understood and interpreted by the organization. Mainly by using mosques, Hamas has built a strong generation of young people who are adherents of Islam. From committed daily prayers and reciting Quranic verses to fighting 'vice' in the street, Hamas members adhere to the finest details of Islamic rituals. The other part of the daily function of Hamas is the struggle against Israel. It is deeply believed in Hamas's thinking that the more devout the individual is, the more self-sacrificing on the battlefield he or she will be. In this way, religious teaching strengthens the liberation front.

The ultimate goals of Hamas are also dual: the 'liberation of Palestine' and the Islamization of society. In the early Hamas thinking and among rigid Palestinian Islamists, these two goals can never be reached simultaneously, but must come in sequence. For them, it would be futile to try to liberate Palestine before achieving a satisfactory degree of Islamization in Palestinian society. To their way of thinking, only religious and Islam-disciplined individuals would be able to defeat Israel. What Hamas has done within that traditional thinking is to break the imagined sequence and argue that both processes can be fought for in parallel. In this, Hamas attracts both those who want to liberate Palestine, and those who want to Islamize Palestinian society.

How far are the nationalists and the religious reconciled within Hamas?

During Hamas's lifetime, the movement has shown a reasonable degree of reconciliation between its nationalist and religious sides. This was helped by the fact that it was in opposition until recently, and never faced the really challenging practical contradictions that arise in the actual practice of governance.

From the nationalist perspective, in the religious aspect of the movement Hamas had mixed fortunes. It maintained extraordinary discipline and a high level of sacrifice from the movement's rank and file with regard to the struggle against Israel. This was the basis for the movement's social solidarity work, which benefited wider Palestinian constituencies, especially in the face of extreme hardship and poverty in refugee camps and deprived areas. Yet at the same time the religious aspect has sometimes taken over the political and nationalist aspect of Hamas at the grassroots level. The major controversial religious practice that Hamas has adopted, directly or indirectly, is the perceived imposition of religious moral codes on Palestinians. In parallel to its rise in influence a quasi-intimidating atmosphere was created particularly in the Gaza Strip, where people felt indirect pressure to comply with Hamas's dictates on moral issues. This issue is discussed in detail in Chapter 5, but the relevant point here is that moves to the forced Islamization of society provoked anger and condemnation among some, at the expense of Hamas's nationalist appeal.

From the religious perspective, the nationalist aspect of the movement also brought Hamas mixed fortunes. In the first place it gave Palestinian Islamists an immensely needed legitimacy, which originated in the mere fact that they were confronting the Israeli occupation. Thus the Palestinian Islamist movement, in its new transformation as Hamas, became bestowed with an additional appeal to reach out to more potential followers and recruits. Moreover, the heavier involvement in the nationalist confrontational effort has broadened the perspectives and experiences of Palestinian Islamists, and brought them to the fore of political realities. This of course propelled the movement to mesh its religious understanding, by way of issuing *fatwas* – religious justifications of successive political and even pseudo-military actions – with the rapid pace of the nationalist struggle and its political requirements. However, the nationalist element was seen as sometimes and in certain ways preaching to or overriding the province of the religious. This has taken place under the surface, in areas such as striking alliances with leftist groups, and participation in politically concerted efforts that could involve agreeing politically on matters that would be disapproved of from the religious viewpoint. For example, in 1996 Hamas boycotted the elections for the Legislative Council, but in 2006 it not only participated in the elections, it won them. This change faced some internal religious disapproval. A minority of voices considered these elections to be *haram* (forbidden) because they involved a compromise over the 'Islamic land of Palestine and Islamic sovereignty over it'.

In summary, Hamas managed to keep its nationalist and religious components somewhat harmonious before taking power in the year 2006. In the post-election era and with Hamas in power, the tension between the religious and the nationalist/political dimensions within the movement started to surface publicly. Immense pressure was thrust on the political leadership of Hamas when, upon unexpectedly winning the elections, it found itself faced almost overnight with hitherto unexperienced challenges. Hamas's government came under immediate international siege, led by the United States and the European Union and involving even the United Nations, not to mention Israel, and this required creative and fast political initiatives. The luxury and time available for formulating every single political step to appease every faction of the internal membership, and for presenting those policies in an appealing format to the outside world as well, have come to an end. It is safe to say that the longer Hamas remains in power, the more tensions will appear between its religious and nationalist constituents, with the probable pragmatic outcome pushing the movement to a more politicized nationalist leaning.

3 Hamas, Israel and Judaism

HAMAS'S VIEW OF THE JEWS

Is Hamas an anti-Semitic movement?

To start with, the term 'anti-Semitic' is highly problematic when it is used to describe Palestinian or Arab perceptions of Jews and Judaism, because Palestinians and Arabs are Semites themselves. Since it is indeed self-contradictory within an Arab context, a more accurate term to describe certain Palestinian and/or Arab attitudes towards Jews might be 'anti-Jewish'.

In their historic context, the indigenous Muslims, Christians and Jews of the Middle East lived together with a remarkable degree of coexistence, particularly when compared with the lack of religious tolerance and the predominance of religious fanaticism in medieval Christian Europe. Jews in particular enjoyed a 'golden era' of centuries-long peaceful living under Islamic rule, in what is known now as the Middle East and North Africa, and particularly in Andalusia. Tolerance toward Jews and Christians in Islamic tradition and societies is underpinned by the *Quran*, where the common roots of Islam, Judaism and Christianity in the Old Testament are acknowledged, and respect for Jews and Christians by Muslims is required. Thus, in principle there is no theological basis for religious (as well as ethnic or racial) discrimination that could lead to European-type anti-Semitism and its manifestations.

Ironically, the strong anti-Jewish feelings that crept into the Middle East by the start of the twentieth century originated in

[31]

Europe, from European ideas compounded by European actions. Since the early twentieth century, European Zionism exploited the ever-growing European desire to resolve the 'Jewish question' (a question astoundingly and notoriously exacerbated by the events of World War II in Nazi-occupied Europe), ultimately by exporting the Jewish populations outside Europe and marrying the solution with the Jewish aspiration of creating a Jewish state in Palestine. With the establishment of Israel by dictat and at the expense of the indigenous Palestinians who had peaceably occupied their lands for over 2000 years, Jews and Zionists, and Judaism and Zionism, became conjoined. With half of the Palestinian people forced out of their homes and lands on the eve of the formation of Israel in 1948, the western-exported Jewry forcibly replaced them, all under the approving eye of Europe and the United States. Thus, the Jews/Zionists came to be seen in the eyes of Palestinians and Arabs as a form of colonial military occupation, consequently destroying the peaceful coexistence of Muslims and Jews that had prevailed in the region for centuries.

The spurious 'anti-Semitic' book *The Protocols of the Elders of Zion* (which also originated in Europe) described the Jews as masterminding a global conspiracy to control the world. It suddenly found a ripe climate in Palestine because of the creation of Israel in the Palestinian homelands in 1948. This date ended the peaceful period of coexistence between Muslims and Jews, and unfolded a new chapter of bloody relationships and hatred.

Unless this background is taken into account, any understanding of the explicit or implicit attitudes in Hamas to Jews is unlikely. Intrinsically and religiously Hamas could not be anti-Jewish. By virtue of Islamic religious teachings, Hamas, or any other Islamic individual or group, is prohibited from inflicting any harm on Jews simply because they are Jews (or Christians, or any other group for that matter). So to be factually correct, Hamas is strongly anti-Zionist, not anti-Jew, with the term Zionist defined as 'a person or group whose focus is the establishment of a Jewish state in Palestine'. (The name comes from Zion, the hill upon which the oldest part of Jerusalem was built.) Although in the early years of its inception Hamas made little effort to differentiate between Judaism as a religion and Zionism as a political movement, in later and recent years Hamas has completely clarified its thinking on this issue. It is anti-Zionist, not anti-Jew.

But surely Hamas's Charter is full of 'anti-Jewish' statements?

It is true that many 'anti-Jewish' statements do exist in the Hamas Charter of 1988. Not only is it also true that years later these statements are irrelevant to the present Hamas party, the Charter itself has become largely obsolete. The Charter was written in early 1988 by one individual and was made public without appropriate general Hamas consultation, revision or consensus, to the regret of Hamas's leaders in later years. The author of the Charter was one of the 'old guard' of the Muslim Brotherhood in the Gaza Strip, completely cut off from the outside world. All kinds of confusions and conflations between Judaism and Zionism found their way into the Charter, to the disservice of Hamas ever since, as this document has managed to brand it with charges of 'anti-Semitism' and a naïve world-view.

Hamas leaders and spokespeople have rarely referred to the Charter or quoted from it, evidence that it has come to be seen as a burden rather than an intellectual platform that embraces the movement's principles. The sophisticated language of the Hamas discourse on the eve of its assuming power after the 2006 elections, and the language and discourse of the Charter of 1988, almost appear to describe two completely different movements.

Indeed, just two years after the publication of the 1988 Charter loaded with anti-Jewish rhetoric, Hamas published documents in 1990 distancing itself from what had been included in the Charter. Emphasizing that its struggle has been merely against Zionists and Zionism, not against the Jews and Judaism, it drew a clear distinction between the two:

> The non-Zionist Jew is one who belongs to the Jewish culture, whether as a believer in the Jewish faith or simply by accident of birth, but ... [who] takes no part in aggressive actions against our land and our nation .... Hamas will not adopt a hostile position in practice against anyone because of his ideas or his creed but will adopt such a position if those ideas and creed are translated into hostile or damaging actions against our people.

Discussing this differentiation with the author, one of Hamas's leaders went so far as to say that 'being Jewish, Zionist or Israeli is irrelevant, what is relevant for me is the notion of occupation and aggression. Even if this occupation was imposed by an Arab or Islamic state and the soldiers were Arabs or Muslims I would resist and fight back.'

On the ground however, in Palestinian cities and refugee camps in the West Bank and the Gaza Strip, ordinary people, including Hamas members, do use the terms 'Jew', 'Zionist' and 'Israeli' interchangeably. On the surface, mixing up these terms blurs the differences: clearly not every Jew is a Zionist, and not every Israeli is a Zionist. However regrettably imprecise the use of any of these terms interchangeably might be in common parlance, it is somewhat irrelevant in the face of the ongoing presence of an aggressive, illegal and Israeli occupier, which whatever distinctions are made is identifiably Jewish (Zionist/Israeli). It is the aggression and occupation that is most relevant, whichever way it gets labelled in the heat of day-to-day confrontation.

Though this should be borne in mind, a type of undeniable anti-Jewishness has come to cut across Palestinian and Arab societies. It is not based on religious, racial or cultural hatred, as in the western rubric 'anti-Semitism'. The roots of any anti-Jewishness in Arab society are entirely political, in response to aggression, and any other form of anti-Jewishness would be completely refuted from the perspective of Islamic theology. Military actions taken against 'Jewish' targets are taken against them as representatives of an illegal, aggressive occupier, and have nothing whatsoever to do with their creed, race or non-Islamic culture.

In Hamas's view, what would be the future of the Jews in Palestine?

Hamas's views on this question are rather vague. In Hamas's early years a standard answer would have been that the Palestinian Jews whose forebears had lived on the land in peace and coexistence with its Muslim inhabitants for centuries would be welcome to stay on in a future Palestinian state. They are, after all, first and foremost Palestinians. Western and other foreign Jews, on the other hand, who had migrated to Palestine from all parts of the world, should return to their countries of origin. In fact this view was commonly shared by Palestinians and Arabs for a long time after the establishment of the state of Israel in 1948, before it gradually faded away. This view has long since been realized to be unrealistic, and has almost completely dropped out of Hamas's discourse. But Hamas has formulated no new answer to fill in the void.

The dilemma that Hamas – and the Palestinian intelli-gentsia at large – have faced concerning this issue is that generations of young Jews with western and worldwide ancestry have been born on historically Palestinian soil as the years of this conflict have dragged on. Of course this is an issue that is part and parcel of the larger 'demographic dimension' to the conflict, which worries both the Palestinians and the Israelis.

Population projections suggest that in the very near future there will be roughly equal numbers of Jews and Palestinians living in the historic land of Palestine. The spectre of demography, and in particular who will overrule whom in the not so distant future, concerns both parties. Israeli solutions have revolved around annexing the maximum amount of Palestinian land with the minimum Palestinian population on it, to preserve the Jewishness of the state in the long run. Palestinian solutions have been to fight to stay on their lands (in the West Bank and the Gaza Strip), defying direct and indirect Israeli measures to force as many of them as possible to leave, and upholding the right to return for refugees whom the Israelis have managed to expel.

Hamas has attempted to break away from the limited thinking that can only imagine Palestinians and Israelis squeezed into 'Palestine/Israel'. A reluctant idea that appears now and then in Hamas's discourse is that Palestine in the future should be part of a wider union of Arab and Muslim territories. In this case, even if the Jews were the majority within the confines of whatever part of historic Palestine they might ultimately claim, they would lose any numerical superority when the remaining territory of Palestine was merged with other Arab territories. The overwhelming Arab majority in the neighbouring countries, who would mix with the population in Palestine, would serve to neutralize the effects of any Jewish majority in Palestine.

A rather less far-fetched view that is, again reluctantly, talked about by Hamas is the one-state solution, based on equality and citizenship, but only if the (more or less 6 million) Palestinian refugees were given the right to return to their cities and villages in Israel. Israel takes no notice of this idea, saying that it would implicitly carry with it the death of the state of Israel by eroding once and for all its Jewish nature and majority.

Hamas, it seems, will have to grapple for a while longer with the question of the future of the Jews in Palestine.

HAMAS'S VIEW OF ISRAEL

What is Israel in Hamas's eyes?

According to Hamas, Israel is a colonial state established by force and resulting from western colonialism and imperialism against Arabs and Muslims before and after the turn of the twentieth century. To the left and right of this central view, there are other perceptions that feed into each other, and sometimes coincide with perceptions held by more secular Palestinian groups. In the early years of its formation Hamas's view of Israel was loaded with religious significance, holding that Israel was the culmination of a Jewish onslaught against Muslims and their holy places in Jerusalem. The establishment of Israel with the strong support of Western powers was seen as a renewal of the medieval Crusades.

The discourse of Hamas has, however, become more developed and adaptive to modern realities. Its views on Israel, accordingly, have been recast within the parameters of occupation/occupier, with the main drive of resistance against Israel directed against its aggression, not its religion. It would be inaccurate to suggest that this development in the discourse of Hamas has sprung from deep roots, or that is has completely replaced the old language, laden with religious antagonism to Israel. But in general parlance the political discourse that is delivered by the Hamas leadership and included in its official statements and documents on Israel is now based mostly on the language of international law, and on political, not religious, assumptions.

Is Hamas planning the destruction of Israel?

The phrase 'the destruction of Israel', as often used by the media when referring to Hamas's 'ultimate goal', is in fact never used or adopted by Hamas, even in its most radical statements. Hamas's ultimate slogan is 'the liberation of Palestine', which falls short of saying what would actually be done with Israel should that goal be achieved. In its rather obsolete Charter issued in early 1988, which is crammed with rhetoric that is embarrassing to the Hamas of today, there are statements that could be interpreted as referring to the destruction of Israel. However, the entire document is of minimal present value, and hardly corresponds to any realities and thinking that Hamas lives and expresses currently.

Realistically speaking, the argument that 'Hamas's tacit and ultimate end is the destruction of Israel' bears no relevance. The facts and positions on the ground speak for themselves, and tend completely in the opposite direction. Neither Hamas nor any other Palestinian or Arab party – or even state for that matter – has any dream of having the ability to destroy Israel. Israel enjoys military capabilities, both conventional and non-conventional, that would enable it to destroy all of its neighbouring countries in the Middle East in a matter of days. It is an uncontested fact that there is no threat to the existence of Israel in either the medium and long term, but there certainly is one against the Palestinians posed by Israel. Depicting Hamas (and the Palestinians) as any such threat to Israel is a matter of political propaganda and emotional sensationalism.

In recent years Hamas has grown out of its early naive discourse of the late 1980s, and today's Hamas projects are more nuanced and its pronouncements more realistic. The dominant theme of its political and military discourse is resistance against the occupation of illegally seized lands and driving the occupiers out of the West Bank and Gaza Strip. Since Hamas took control of the Palestinian Authority after elections in 2006 it has not expressed a single word of the old rhetoric of the Charter, or issued any ill-considered slogans.

In summary, any suggestion that Hamas plans or aims to destroy Israel is obviously naive. For Hamas to be able to achieve such a goal it would have to remain in power for decades, defeating all the Palestinian groups that would not work toward that goal. It would also have to build a massive Palestinian army in the West Bank and the Gaza Strip over decades, with Israel unconcernedly looking on. It would have to import tanks and jet fighters, from sympathetic international sources that do not exist, and train hundreds of thousands of soldiers on the tiny strips of non-contiguous land it would control. How could Hamas possibly defeat Israel militarily, let alone destroy it, when all other Arab countries collectively have failed to do so in the past half-century?

Despite what euphoria Hamas has seemed to enjoy at its high peaks, both militarily in its waves of successful suicide attacks in the heart of Israeli cities, and politically in its election victory in 2006, Hamas remains defensive rather than offensive. The structural confines that limit Palestinians in general apply to Hamas as well, and sometimes even more so because of the specificity of the movement (such as the lack of international support, unlike the case with the PLO). Wary of its difficult position, Hamas's engagement in politics and world affairs is mostly driven by defensive mechanisms. Its ultimate goal in the coming years will be simply to preserve its own existence and avoid destruction, not to destroy others.

Would Hamas ever recognize Israel and conclude peace agreements with it?

It is not inconceivable that Hamas would recognize Israel. Hamas's pragmatism and its realistic approach to issues leave ample room for such a development. Yet most of the conditions that could create a conducive climate for such a step lie in the hands of the Israelis. As long as Israel refuses to acknowledge the basic rights of the Palestinian people in any end result based on the principle of a two-state solution, it is inconceivable that Hamas will recognize Israel.

Despite the often-cited rhetoric in Hamas's discourse about the impossibility of recognizing Israel, there actually is a visible thread of thinking that offers just such a possibility, though only if Israel reciprocated positively. After assuming his new post in early April 2006, Hamas's foreign minister Mahmoud al-Zahhar sent a letter to Kofi Annan, the Secretary-General of the United Nations, declaring that his government would be willing to live in peace, side by side with 'its neighbours', based on a two-state solution. However, other statements attributed to Hamas leaders have implied that the issue of recognizing Israel should be one of the goals of negotiations, not the prerequisite to them.

If Israel shows no interest in dealing with Hamas, and insists on 'unilateral measures' that perpetuate the occupational status quo, Hamas will never recognize Israel. If this were to be the only proffered political climate, the maximum that the movement could accept would be a long-term truce, and it would avoid and evade recognizing Israel to the end.

That a peace treaty could be concluded between Israel and

Hamas, however, is not implausible. Hamas enjoys influence, legitimacy and a clean record in governance among the Palestinians, furnishing it with the political capital needed to negotiate with Israel. Attempting to find some leeway between its past declarations about non-recognition of Israel and the pressing realities at hand, the movement has created a distinction between the government of Hamas and Hamas as an organization. Implicitly, this means that Hamas's government is ready to go beyond the standard and well-known declarations of Hamas as a party. Yet again, the extent to which Hamas could go down the course of negotiating with Israel is strongly contingent on the positions offered by the latter.

To reconcile the extreme of the liberation of the entire historic land of Palestine with the realities of the existence of Israel on the ground, Hamas has suggested resorting to a national referendum on the final settlement to be concluded by Israel and the Palestinians. The democratically elected Hamas will abide by whatever the Palestinian people decide concerning their own fate, in a free and democratic referendum. By Hamas's way of thinking, the referendum idea is a decent solution to the theoretical and practical impasse that could result, and be exclusively, if wrongly, put down to Hamas's refusal to recognize Israel and accept the principle of a two-state solution. If peace talks led to the drafting of a peace treaty that required the 'negotiating parties' to recognize each other (and it was a treaty in which Palestinian rights were acknowledged and granted in a manner likely to be satisfactory to the Palestinians), then Hamas would accept any decision taken by the people on such a treaty via the mechanism of a referendum. Hamas as an organization says publicly that under such conditions it would have no choice but to respect the will and decision endorsed by the Palestinian people.

4 Hamas's resistance and military strategy

FORCING UNCONDITIONAL ISRAELI WITHDRAWAL

What is Hamas's 'program(me) of resistance'?

'Resistance' as a concept is the most central principle in the thinking and formation of Hamas; it is even part of its very name, 'the Islamic Resistance Movement'. When Hamas was established in late 1987, the Palestinian and Arab political climate was still absorbing the shock created by Egypt's recognition of Israel and the peace treaty concluded by both countries in 1982. Negotiation, rather than armed struggle, was being put forward emphatically as a means to achieve political goals, including the restoration of occupied land. In the same year of 1982, the PLO was defeated by Israel in Lebanon and consequently all Palestinian guerrillas and their leadership were forced to leave the country and move to Tunis. The logic of using armed resistance to liberate Palestine had thus suffered two major blows in one year. Since then, and with the new North African PLO base very far from Palestine, a strategy of peace negotiations and initiatives started to dominate over the armed struggle approach. The PLO itself became far more lenient than before on the issue of negotiation with Israel and the principle of a two-state solution.

[43]

By contrast, in reiterating and reaffirming the concept of 'resistance' Hamas was declaring its position against any negotiated settlement with Israel, and injecting new blood in a somewhat fading concept. The only way to regain Palestinian rights, Hamas vehemently suggested with rising confidence, was through resistance against the colonial occupation and wresting back rights from the enemy. Hamas's logic came down to the idea that wherever a military occupation exists, a military resistance should be expected. Such resistance, in all its various forms, would only stop when the occupation ended.

All Hamas's conduct, policies and actions emanate from and are justified by this conviction. However, there have been few specific details offered about how matters would proceed beyond this concept, particularly on how the 'withdrawal' of the occupying troops would take place, or what would follow it. Hamas's leaders have kept repeating, 'Withdraw first, and then we take things as they come.'

This 'strategy' of Hamas, which in effect spells out no long-term strategy, might appear on the surface to be futile and shallow. Yet, at a more fundamental level, it has proved successful and pragmatic for the organization. First, its plain terminology and uncompromising simplicity have been hard to argue against; second, this same single focus and simplicity conceals Hamas's theological arguments, which are more difficult to sell; third, it provides an uncomplicated theoretical umbrella under which Hamas's military and non-military actions of 'resistance' can easily be conducted.

Throughout Hamas's lifetime, beginning in late 1987, various forms of resistance have been deployed, ranging from popular uprisings, mobilization, strikes, and military attacks against the Israeli army and settlers, to executing suicide bombings in the heart of Israeli cities. These have been deployed either in combination or separately, but in all cases using whichever method has corresponded to the specific political environment prevailing at the time. The ultimate aim of any combination of all sorts of resistance, in Hamas's thinking, is to force unconditional Israeli withdrawal. The struggle of all Palestinian organizations, including of course the PLO and its factions, and the Palestinian Authority which was established in the West Bank and Gaza Strip in 1993/4, has been focused on achieving such a withdrawal. However, Hamas wants it without surrendering any other Palestinian rights in return, and without the recognition of Israel. The PLO and other Palestinian factions have come to terms with a reciprocal recognition with Israel based on the two-state solution. Hamas will not accept this, but might accept a formula that tacitly recognizes the de facto existence of Israel but without formally recognizing any right of Israel to exist. This is because regardless of whether the withdrawal resulted directly from peace talks or by force, Hamas could logically insist that it takes place without compromising any additional Palestinian rights, or issues such as sovereignty over East Jerusalem, the position of borders and the right of Palestinian refugees to return.

How has Hamas's 'programme of resistance' materialized on the ground?

Hamas believes that the unilateral Israeli withdrawal from the Gaza Strip in 2005 validates its strategy of resistance. Various declarations by Hamas representatives have stated that the withdrawal was the result, to a large part if not fully, of the continuous resistance and long-term pressure on the Israeli troops and settlers in the Strip, which left Israel with no option but to yield and withdraw. Many other Palestinians, however, refute this view and call into suspicion Israel's real purpose and intention in taking this step. They fear that Israel has withdrawn from the Gaza Strip, which has no strategic or religious value to the Jewish state, in order to concentrate and consolidate its occupation and control over the West Bank and Jerusalem, where the true battle between the Palestinians and the Israelis lies.

In the West Bank, too, Hamas believes that carrying out cycles of confrontation against the occupation will make the cost of the Israeli presence there unsustainable; that multiplying Israeli costs in terms of human loss, draining of resources, mounting internal tension and deteriorating image worldwide will eventually bear fruit. When upon winning the Israeli elections in March 2006 the Kadima party made public its intention to undertake unilateral partial withdrawals from certain areas in the West Bank, Hamas claimed part of the credit. It argued, again, that had there been no resistance with costly consequences to Israel, any withdrawal, however small, would have only been undertaken in return for excessive Palestinian concessions.

It is worth mentioning that Hamas points to the experience of Hizbullah, which was perceived to have forced Israel to withdraw unconditionally from south Lebanon in 2000. At that time the Israeli step was taken for a variety of reasons, including the diminishing chances of the Israeli occupation in that area achieving any strategic objectives, and the mounting questioning of the value of that occupation by Israeli decision makers and the Israeli public as well. That of course was in addition to the continuous, conspicuous and highly emotive daily losses, notably on the side of Israeli soldiers. Hizbullah naturally chose to focus on this last factor exclusively, to vindicate its 'resistance strategy'. Likewise, Hamas has underlined the same factor, calling Palestinians to emulate Hizbullah in exerting extreme pressure on the Israeli occupation to force unilateral withdrawal.

What is the intifada *(as in the first* intifada *of 1987 and the second* intifada *of 2000)?*

Intifada is the Arabic word for a popular uprising. Within the Palestinian context it evokes sentimental connotations, since popular uprisings, or *intifadas*, typically and historically marked certain turning points in the course of the Palestinian national struggle in the past decades. During the British mandate over Palestine (1922–48), Palestinian uprisings were directed against the British, with the most significant one occurring in 1936.

In the era of the Israeli occupation *intifadas* were almost the only effective means at the disposal of the Palestinians. Apart from small-scale uprisings and forms of resistance, the two major *intifadas* erupted in 1987 and 2000. The 1987 uprising took place initially in the Gaza Strip on 8 December, then the spark moved to the cities of the West Bank. The causes that led to the *intifada* were multifold and fed off each other. They were the escalation of brutality by the Israeli occupation, and the growing anger among Palestinians in response to the humiliation of the occupation – not only politically, but in the very real way that the occupation had reduced those areas to soul-destroying poverty – and the rising power of the Islamists, who were compelled to adopt a new confrontational policy against Israel, as has been discussed earlier in the book.

The immediate causes that actually ignited the *intifada* were a series of events linked to the escape of a number of Palestinian prisoners who hid in one of the refugee camps, then killed an Israeli settler. In response to the killing, an Israeli truck ran down some Palestinian workers, killing four and wounding nine others. Consequently, angry Palestinians took to the streets of the Gaza Strip in the following days in unprecedented mass demonstrations. If the early days of the *intifada* were spontaneous with no organizational planning behind them, the following days witnessed heavy engagement and even rivalry between the Palestinian organizations, including the newly established Hamas, to spearhead the *intifada* and keep it going.

The 1987 *intifada* was mostly a weaponless confrontation, relying instead on mobilizing people, mass demonstrations and throwing stones at Israeli soldiers. Hence it was called the 'stones revolution'. It did not witness the practice of suicide bombing, which was a couple more years in coming. Erratically waxing and waning, the *intifada* lasted roughly until 1993 when the Oslo Accords were signed between Israel and the PLO, resulting for the first time in a Palestinian form of authority in the West Bank and the Gaza Strip.

The second *intifada* took place in September 2000. The causes behind this *intifada* were somewhat different. After seven years of the Oslo Accords with Israel, which had promised the Palestinians a sovereign and independent state by the end of the year 1999, the Palestinian public lost confidence in the process and became frustrated. Through those Accords it had been hoped that an interim period of five years, starting in 1993, would end in resolving the major issues of the conflict including Jerusalem, the control of borders, dismantling the Israeli settlements in the West Bank and the Gaza Strip, and the status of refugees.

Contrary to those hopes, all evidence pointed to the fact that the Israeli occupation was tightening its grip, and that the newly set-up Palestinian authority was being restricted in effect to administrating much of the occupation – from the prosaic daily services of the population, to actually maintaining the security of Israel and its settlers from Palestinian attacks. The size and population of Israeli settlements on land that was supposed to have been returned to the Palestinians almost doubled during the years following the Oslo Agreement. The status of Jerusalem, a major issue of the conflict yet to be resolved in negotiation, was swept under heavier Israeli control. By the eve of the second *intifada*, the peace process brought about by the Oslo Accords was witnessing the first signs of its own demise.

The immediate spark of the 2000 *intifada* was Ariel Sharon's provocative visit to al-Harm al-Shirif, the holiest Muslim site in Jerusalem, which infuriated Palestinians. Against much advice Sharon, then the leader of the Likud opposition party, decided to make a point for political purposes against the ruling Israeli Labour party, that even the holiest of Muslim places in Jerusalem were under full Israeli control and jurisdiction.

Although it started as a popular uprising with no use of weapons, the second *intifada* quickly turned into an armed confrontation. Palestinians across the political spectrum supported the *intifada*: the ruling PA organizations, such as Fatah and other PLO factions, stood side by side with Hamas and other opposition factions.

Will Hamas disarm itself voluntarily or be disarmed at all forcibly if needed?

'What you get from anyone, or on a negotiating table should match your strength on the ground', Sheikh Ahmad Yassin, the founder of Hamas, was once quoted as saying. 'Strength' is interpreted in all forms, with the military figures on the top. Thus, since its inception in late 1987, Hamas (and other Palestinian factions) have amassed considerable caches of weapons mainly in the Gaza Strip but also in the West Bank. These include machine guns, bombs, and homemade rockets with a range of a few kilometres and capable of striking Israeli settlements if launched from parts of the Gaza Strip.

In terms of quality, quantity and military effectiveness, Hamas's weapons, and all other Palestinian weapons combined for that matter, have never amounted to a serious threat to the state of Israel. These weapons could only inflict harm in the form of guerrilla attacks, quick and short shootouts and suicide bombings. Sources for acquiring weaponry include smuggling it in from Egypt (against the policy of the Egyptian government of course), and buying Israeli weapons from 'black markets' and from discontented individuals in the Palestinian security forces who were armed officially by the Palestinian Authority. Hamas has also developed local manufacture of primitive weapons, notably bombs and short-range rockets, based on domestic material.

During and after the second *intifada* of 2000, it was obvious that Hamas's military power had reached new peaks, particularly in the Gaza Strip, paralleling that of the Palestinian Authority. On the eve of its landslide victory in the January 2006 elections in the West Bank and the Gaza Strip, it was believed that Hamas's arsenal of weapons could furnish the movement with the enormous leverage that goes hand in hand with its political and popular influence.

There is significant consensus among observers that Hamas's weaponry, used and supervised by its military wing Izzedin al-Qassam, is under the tight control of the movement. Apart from a few factional incidents where Hamas members used weapons, their use is strictly limited to the struggle with Israel. Also, this weaponry has clearly provided Hamas with a deterrent against other Palestinian rivals, mainly the Fatah movement and the Palestinian Authority.

The situation in the Gaza Strip has been marked by chaos and a multiplicity of centres of power since the eruption of the first *intifada* in 1987. Accessibility to arms has created a hard-to-control environment, and factional rivalry has brought Palestinians to the verge of civil war on more than one occasion. When the Palestinian Authority was established in 1993/4 one of its main responsibilities, pressed on it by Israel under the Oslo Accords, was to control the chaotic situation and unify the 'Palestinian arms' under its control. Stridently, Hamas refused any proposal to hand in its weapons to the Palestinian Authority, or any suggestion in the direction of giving the Palestinian Authority the slightest supervision over its weapons.

Ironically, when Hamas came to power after winning the elections of January 2006 and itself became the Palestinian Authority, it called upon other factions to unite their armed wings under one unified control under the supervision of Hamas in its new PA role. As was to be expected, Fatah's military wing and other factions refused Hamas's call.

In the short and medium terms, it is neither likely that Hamas would disarm voluntarily, nor conceivable that it could be disarmed forcibly by other parties (including Israel and other Palestinian groups). Hamas keeps repeating its position that its arms are there to defend the Palestinian people and their rights, and insofar as Israeli continues to occupy Palestinian land, and those rights are not realized, armed struggle and all it entails should stay at the heart of Hamas, and thus at the moment, of official Palestinian strategy.

SUICIDE ATTACKS

When and why has Hamas adopted suicide bombing as a strategy?

Hamas's suicide attacks against Israeli civilians are justified by public statements made by its officials now and then, stating that these attacks are reciprocal actions. They are generated,

Hamas says, in response to the Israeli killing of Palestinian civilians, and will end immediately once Israel declares that it will stop doing the same to Palestinians. Offers of negotiation by Hamas were made to save civilians from both sides of the targeted killing, but met with categorical refusal from Israel on the grounds that it would 'do no business with terrorists'.

Although Hamas came into being in 1987, its trademark suicide attacks did not begin until 1994. The first wave of these attacks was carried out in retaliation for the Hebron massacre, in which a fanatic Israeli settler killed 29 Palestinian worshipers in the Abrahimic Mosque in February 1994. Hamas vowed to take revenge and it did so by blowing up Israeli soldiers, settlers and civilians in the hearts of Israeli cities. At that point Hamas discovered the spectacular effect this kind of attack had on the public imagination, and embraced it. Realizing that targeting civilians deliberately can be a dangerous strategy, Hamas has been careful to link any suicide bombing that it has undertaken to specific Israeli killings of Palestinian civilians.

Prior to 1994 Hamas's policies were clear in attacking only 'legitimate military targets'. The major shift to targeting civilians, even with the justification of only retaliating for a civilian killing with another civilian killing, has nonetheless incurred heavy costs to Hamas. Defying Israel's violent retaliation against Hamas, epitomized by the Israeli strategy of assassinating its leaders, the movement has geared up its use of suicide operations over the years. It had realized that although these operations rallied the international community against Hamas, and distorted somewhat the image of the legitimate Palestinian struggle, they provided the movement with an aura of strength and popularity amongst the Palestinian people themselves. The Palestinians started to look at Hamas as an organization capable of inflicting damage on the Israelis and taking revenge for any Israeli killing of Palestinians.

Lacking any effective means to defend its civilians against these suicide attacks, Israel was devastated by them. The horror of a potential bombing that could take place in any bus, shopping centre or restaurant brought Israeli cities at certain periods of time nearly to complete state of terrifying suspense. Israel not only mobilized its military might to stamp out Hamas's infrastructure in the Gaza Strip and the West Bank, but also brought to bear all sorts of pressure, including external pressure. On more than one occasion Israel hinted, via unofficial mediators, that it was ready to talk to Hamas with a view to stopping these attacks. However Hamas adhered to its declared position: 'Stop killing Palestinian civilians and we will stop killing Israeli civilians.' Israel repeatedly refused this offer.

Sheikh Yasin succinctly articulated Hamas's policy on suicide bombings in September 2003. When asked whether the attacks would continue irrespective of circumstances, he replied in the negative, and explained, 'If we perceive that the atmosphere favors such a decision, we stop. And when we perceive that the atmosphere has changed, we carry on.' In general, the wider the gap between the peace strategy and the attainment of Palestinian rights, the more room Hamas has to pursue its resistance strategy.

Politically and strategically, Hamas became aware that, at certain junctures, using suicide attacks had become its strongest card in the conflict with Israel, as well as with its rivalry with the Palestinian Authority and its Fatah movement. Relinquishing this card would only be considered if there was really a possibility of a worthy return. Continuous Israeli military efforts, coupled with repetitive crackdowns on Hamas by the security forces of the Palestinian Authority, failed to destroy Hamas's capability in undertaking these attacks. Political and diplomatic pressures were also exerted on Hamas by Egypt, Jordan and the European Union in order to compel the movement to stop these attacks, at least temporarily. In finding itself on the receiving end of much high condemnation for the suicide bombings both regionally and internationally, Hamas discovered that the exact same attention regionally and internationally was also furnishing them with further leverage.

On several occasions Hamas has shown flexibility in temporarily halting its attacks, either to avoid straying from a collective agreement among Palestinian factions, or to prove its pragmatism. In late 1995 it stopped suicide attacks for months, only to resume them after the Israeli assassination of one of its· military leaders, Yahya Ayyash. Similar halt–resume 'tacit agreements' took place during the second *intifada* (2000–05) for short periods of time, but all failed because Israel would waste no opportunity to assassinate one Hamas leader after another.

How many Israelis has Hamas killed? And how many Hamas members have the Israelis killed or imprisoned?

Hamas's suicide attacks have given the movement a bad name by enabling Israel to succeed in selling an image of Hamas as a mere 'terrorist organisation' whose sole purpose is the killing of innocent Israeli civilians. The justness of the Palestinian cause has paid a high price because of them, as Israel has exploited the attacks by reducing the nature of the Palestinian struggle to an issue of 'terrorism and counter-terrorism'. The worldwide condemnation of the Palestinian killing of Israelis is gravely uneven compared with the mild condemnation of similar Israeli killings of Palestinians. The number of Israelis killed by Hamas (and all other Palestinian factions combined) from Hamas's inception in December 1987 until April 2006 amounted to only a quarter of the number of the Palestinians killed by Israel over the same period of time.

The killing of civilians on both sides is inhumane, and to deal with dead civilians as mere statistics implies a measure of insensitivity. Yet the statistics help to further the understanding of the whole picture. The aggregate figures of the statistics provided by the Israeli human rights organisation Btselem (www.btselem.org) show that 1,426 Israelis, military personnel and civilians, were killed by Palestinian factions, compared with 5,050 Palestinians killed by Israel during those years. Of those casualties, there were 137 Israeli children (or under 18) killed against 998 Palestinian children of the same age group.

What is the truce (hudna) that Hamas offers?

Hamas's defiance of both continuous Israeli attacks and mounting international criticism against its suicide operations has been accompanied by the offer of a *hudna* – the religious Islamic concept of the classical notion of a truce, though with certain differences – with the aim of easing pressure. The *hudna* is a rather flexible traditional Islamic war practice which was first used by the Prophet Muhammad in the famous Hodaibiya *hudna,* when in 628 AD he concluded with his enemies a ten-year truce, during which people of the two parties were to live in peace. Later in Islamic history *hudna* were used by different rulers to achieve different goals, hence the flexibility and broad meaning of the concept. The debate remains open among Muslim scholars whether the *hudna* concept is merely a tactical ceasefire or a more sophisticated practice which lays the groundwork for non-violent solutions.

Bound by its religious roots, Hamas has felt the need to justify its adoption of any controversial policy on Islamic religious grounds. Hamas's offer of a truce would seem to

[55]

contradict its leading principle of *Jihad* – military struggle – against Israel. Similarly, refraining from military struggle was the approach that was officially adopted by the PLO and the Palestinian Authority and which ended in peace negotiations with Israel which were, in turn, strongly opposed by Hamas. To yield to a ceasefire Hamas would be seen to be simply following in the footsteps of its rivals, risking the loss of its distinctiveness.

Thus, by offering the *hudna* Hamas has been very keen to distinguish this concept from the practice of the PLO and the Palestinian Authority, which has always been described by Hamas as capitulation. There are two main distinctions that Hamas draws between a ceasefire and a *hudna*. The first is that a *hudna* is only an agreement on halting hostilities, not a peace treaty which could comprise concessions, and the second is that a ceasefire has lately come to imply an open-ended agreement whereas the *hudna* is limited by a period of time that is agreed between the belligerent parties. If the PLO and the Palestinian Authority are ready to abandon armed struggle and promote a lasting ceasefire, Hamas is not ready to do the same. The furthest that it could do, the *hudna* argument runs, is to agree on ten or 20 years of ceasefire without compromising on Palestinian rights. The *hudna* would calm down the situation, end violence and save the blood of civilians. The question, of course, is what would happen after the *hudna*? Hamas's answer is that the next step would depend on the acceptable behaviour of Israel and its intentions: the *hudna* could be renewed or ended.

On several separate occasions, Hamas has offered a *hudna* to Israel. The late Sheikh Ahmad Yasin was the first to suggest the idea back in 1993. Since then Hamas figures have repeated the offer, sometimes changing the period of time that it included (ten, 20 or even 30 years). Israel has always ridiculed the offer, yet some Israeli politicians conceive it to represent a pragmatic element in Hamas that should be encouraged. When Hamas came to power and controlled the Palestinian Authority in January 2006, it renewed its offer of a *hudna* to Israel for from ten to 20 years.

5 Hamas's political and social strategy

HAMAS'S POSITION ON THE VARIOUS PEACE PLANS WITH ISRAEL

Why does Hamas reject the peace agreements reached by the PLO and Israel in 1993/4, known as the Oslo Accords?

The original Palestinian position concerning the creation of Israel in 1948 was a complete Palestinian consensus to reject any proposal that would situate Israel on any part of the historic land of Palestine. This position remained almost unchanged until 1988, when the Palestine Liberation Organization (PLO) publicly declared its readiness to accept the concept of a two-state solution: Palestine in the West Bank and Gaza Strip (less than a quarter of historic Palestine) and Israel in the rest of the land. By then Israel would not even entertain the proposal, and none of the major Israeli parties accepted that concept officially until very late in 2006 when the two-state solution was adopted by Ehud Olmert's Kadima party.

The balance of power has constantly favoured Israel, which has always enjoyed unreserved support from the United States and the West. Israel was thus under no pressure to even acknowledge the resolutions issued by the United Nations supporting the two-state solution and calling on Israel to withdraw from the territories it has occupied since the 1967 war.

The Oslo Agreements in 1993/4 offered the Palestinians limited self-rule but only over the Palestinian population – with no real jurisdiction over Palestinian land – for five years, as a testing period. Should the Palestinians show 'good behaviour' then negotiations would be initiated to settle the major issues of the conflict, such as the fate or division of Jerusalem (which both 'states' claim as their rightful capital), the status of refugees, the dismantling of Jewish settlements in the West Bank and the Gaza Strip, control of borders and full sovereignty. From the Palestinian viewpoint, throughout the 'test period' the situation surrounding all the major contested issues has been exacerbated deliberately by Israel so that the resulting confrontational disorder would fail to meet the minimal requirements for any restitution of Palestinian rights. From the Israeli perspective, the Palestinians have clearly failed to prove that they are fit to be a 'partner' in peace, and thus no advancement should be undertaken to jointly solve the conflict.

Hamas's view has been that the Oslo Agreements, and any peace talks for that matter, are worthless as long as their design is built around a balance of power where the fulfilment of Israeli demands tops the agenda. According to Hamas, these are capitulation treaties, not peace agreements. From Hamas's perspective, the failure of the Oslo Accords is inevitable and the rationale behind this goes as follows:

> Oslo proponents claimed for months following its sign-
> ing that it would bring an end to occupation [of Pales-
> tine] and that, therefore, the Palestinians need no longer
> exercise an armed struggle against the Israelis. But eight
> years after Oslo, the following have been the dividends
> of peace:
> 1. The territories occupied in 1967 are still occupied.
> 2. More than ever, the West Bank and Gaza have been

carved up, mutilated and turned into isolated islands of human concentrations, or cantons, administered on behalf of the Israelis by the Palestinian Authority.

3. Existing illegal Jewish settlements continue to expand and new ones have been erected.

4. Jerusalem is being expanded and de-Arabised.

5. Large areas of land have been confiscated to allow for the construction of by-passes for the exclusive use of Jewish motorists and especially settlers who illegally live on confiscated Arab land.

6. Thousands of Palestinians continue to be detained in Israeli prisons.

7. Various forms of collective punishment continue to be adopted by the Israelis including the demolition of Palestinian homes, the closure of entire areas and the enforcement of economic blockades, the destruction of Palestinian infrastructure and the uprooting of trees and crops.

8. The economic situation for Palestinians is more dire than ever before.

In other words, the peace process has not improved by one iota the conditions of Palestinians under occupation and does not seem to promise any better future. The claim that armed struggle was no longer necessary (it should be noted here that no one within the Palestinian camp ever agreed that resistance was illegal) has been refuted by reality, giving credence to the Hamas argument (which is no different from the argument adopted before Oslo by the nationalist movement as a whole and that continues to be adopted by a score of Palestinian factions opposed to Oslo) that armed struggle is the only real means of liberation.

Hamas claims that by refusing ill-designed peace processes it upholds Palestinian rights and remains their defender. Hamas's opponents and critics in Palestinian circles and beyond say that the movement has not only offered no alternative, but was partly if not mostly responsible for the failure of the peace process when it continued its military attacks against Israel.

Popular referenda as a political programme

The political dilemma that Hamas has faced emanates from a realistic assumption: what is the reality if the majority of Palestinians accept a peace treaty with Israel that is still rejected by Hamas? If Hamas is adamant in staying true to its own principles, which consider peace treaties predominantly predicated on Israeli terms as akin to surrender, it is equally anxious to remain connected to and representative of the desires and aspirations of the majority of Palestinians. The solution to this dilemma was offered by Hamas through the idea of a referendum. This would mean that any form of final solution based on a negotiated settlement should be reached through a Palestinian consensus, which is achievable only by holding a referendum for all Palestinians inside and outside Palestine under international supervision.

In calling for a referendum Hamas wants more than to just rally the general Palestinian public into becoming strongly involved in deciding their own destiny. The movement is more concerned that at some point it will face the hard choice between continuing the armed struggle against the general mood of the Palestinian public, or becoming a purely political party. The referendum idea gives legitimacy to any future decision on the part of Hamas to abandon its armed activities. At the same time a collective popular vote on the final settlement would work to place the negotiating process and its results or compromises under bold popular scrutiny. This scrutiny, Hamas could then be assured, would surely be based on the preservation of Palestinian rights.

ELECTIONS, DEMOCRACY AND MOBILIZATION

Is Hamas genuinely democratic?

This is a standard rhetorical question which is always waved in the face of Islamist movements in the Middle East and elsewhere. There is little historic experience upon which one can judge accurately whether these movements have adopted democratic practices wholeheartedly. The same lack of actual history should also allow some benefit of the doubt. In the Middle Eastern context the question applies equally to all parties regardless of their political ideology. Democratic practice is visibly in short supply, and in the postcolonial era in the region there have been almost no fully fledged democracies. In Arab republics, nationalist and socialist parties have come to power, by either elections or military coups, and have never relinquished power peacefully. In Arab monarchies, changing the system by democratic means has been out of the question. Thus, questioning how authentically democratic the Islamist movements are, in an environment that lacks democracy, implies considerable accusation as a starting point. In all the cases in the Middle East where ruling parties rejected democracy, or dismissed the results of elections because an opposition party won the majority, the intransigents were non-Islamist parties.

Therefore, Hamas is as genuine in its democratic conviction as any other political party, in a region inexperienced in this form of governance. There are, however, certain specificities in the make-up of Hamas that could help in exploring the level of its democratic credibility. Internally, the movement has embraced democratic practices in choosing its leaders. These practices have been well established and have even stretched less practicably to areas where democratic consensus might not have brought about ideal results. For example, when Hamas was in the process of forming its government in March 2006, the prime minister and all the cabinet ministers were elected by the rank and file. In the process, Hamas's cabinet ended up with a team of ministers that was not necessarily composed of the best people for their responsibilities. Instead of mandating the prime minister to form his government as a working unit based on professional and political considerations, all of the individual ministers were imposed on him in a democratic but perhaps more shambolic fashion from the party floor. It would appear that it could be safely said that there is no authoritarian system within Hamas as a party. In most cases, and at least in the Middle Eastern context, parties with authoritarian internal practices tend to import these qualities into their governments when they come to power.

It also must be remembered that Hamas has always defined itself as a resistance movement, essentially preoccupied with confronting the Israeli military occupation of Palestine. This occupation, with all its military resources, has always held the upper hand in this conflict, and controls every aspect of sovereignty over what has been left of any Palestinian state. All internal Palestinian politics take place under that control, and being voted in to take charge of a Palestinian government that functions under ultimate Israeli rule is hardly a great enticement to Hamas. Specifically because of the parameters of this foreign military control, Hamas never aspired to, or planned to, win a majority in any Palestinian elections, since this would have forced it into such an awkward position. Hamas's victory in the 2006 elections caught the movement by surprise, and it is hard to imagine Hamas wishing to cling to this awkward position by blocking or manipulating any coming elections. Given the 'siege' of protest and censure that it faces regionally and internationally, Hamas's biggest challenge will be to avoid total collapse and finish its four-year term in government with the least possible losses. Any scenario that has Hamas manoeuvering to remain in such a compromised position of power by force is highly unlikely.

Within the Palestinian polity, especially in the post-Yasser Arafat era, the Palestinian political environment is not receptive to any kind of authoritarian rule. The centres of power have been fragmented and Hamas is at loggerheads with its rivals, particularly the Fatah movement. If Hamas decided to remain in power contrary to democratic practices, the immediate internecine result would be severe. Furthermore, the diversity of Palestinian society, the high level of education, and the general envy of the 'Israeli democracy' next door, narrow down any possibility of the development of an undemocratic Hamas. Secular, leftist and liberal lines of thought have been historically engraved all over Palestinian society, no less upon the powerful Palestinian Christian community, which is highly politicized and active. Thus, even if Hamas wanted to opt for any undemocratic form of politics the surrounding internal circumstances would abort that option.

What is the significance of Hamas's winning the Palestinian elections of January 2006, and why did the Palestinians vote for Hamas?

Hamas's triumph in the 2006 elections was a complete shock for all parties concerned, including Hamas itself. Hamas's plan was to win a large enough number of seats, around 40 to 45 per cent, to enable it to play the role of the guardian of the Palestinian

[65]

people's rights but without bearing the direct and ultimate responsibility of the government, which because of the Israeli control was highly undesirable. The general thinking was by winning this share of seats Hamas would easily form coalitions with other smaller leftist opposition groups and would be capable of blocking any future compromises made by Fatah. The 'dirty' business of day-to-day governing would still have been left to Fatah, but it would have been hobbled politically in its negotiations with Israel. The outcome of the elections, however, was a landslide victory, with Hamas winning almost 60 per cent of the seats. The defeat of Fatah was resounding.

The reasons behind the Hamas victory are multiple. In the first place the movement harvested long years of devoted work and popularity among Palestinians. At least half of the voters supported Hamas outright for its programmes and declared objectives. The other half were driven by other forces. The failure of the peace process combined with the ever-increasing Israeli brutality had left Palestinians with no faith in negotiating a peaceful settlement with Israel. The balance in the debate surrounding peace talks versus resistance was teetering, as the date for the elections came nearer and nearer. The notion of 'peace talks' was clearly losing ground, but there was no clear and definite support for the 'resistance' concept. The latter was vague, and many Palestinians were wary about its meaning and mechanisms. But the frustration of the peace talks took its toll and contributed largely to the defeat of the Fatah movement, the main force behind and upholder of the Oslo Accords and all that resulted from them.

Another major factor that helped Hamas in winning these elections was the failure in almost all areas of the Fatah-led Palestinian Authority. Not only did it fail externally in the peace talks with Israel, it also failed miserably internally, in managing the daily lives of the Palestinian people. Mismanagement, corruption and theft were the 'attributes' that came to be used to describe top leaders, ministers and their high-ranking staff. As unemployment and poverty reached unprecedented levels, the extravagant lifestyle of senior Palestinian officials infuriated the public, and it was the elections that empowered the people to punish those officials. Thus the elections proved to be the reaping season for both Hamas in its victory, and Fatah in its defeat.

It is easy to refute any suggestion that the Palestinian people voted for Hamas primarily on religious grounds. There was certainly no overnight popular conviction in favour of Hamas's religious or even political ideology. Christians and secular people voted for Hamas in various constituencies side by side with Hamas members and exponents. Hamas members also supported Christian candidates and won them seats in the parliament. Hamas itself appointed a Christian to its cabinet as the minister of tourism. The diverse nature of Hamas's voters confirmed that people were voting for Hamas as the nationalist liberation movement that promised change and reform on all fronts.

The victory itself is of paramount significance not only for Palestinians but also for Arabs, Muslims and beyond. At the Palestinian level it is a historic turning point, where a major shift in leadership has taken place. For the first time in more than half a century an Islamist group – grounded in national liberation – has moved into the driver's seat, replacing the secular leadership that had controlled Palestine's destiny and national decision-making process for decades. This fundamental change, furthermore, was realized through peaceful means and without violence, giving Hamas and all Palestinians a great sense of pride that they have embraced democracy and respect its outcome. It also gave them the chance to revisit the strategy over the conflict with Israel, which had been designed and pursued by the Fatah movement. For Hamas, this victory has represented the greatest challenge that the movement has faced since its inception. Almost overnight, all Hamas's ideals and slogans have been brought down to face realities on the ground. It could be safely said that the post-elections Hamas will be considerably different from the one before them.

At the Arab and Muslim level, Hamas's victory has been almost unique in that political Islam finally reached power, and in a democratic way. Islamist movements in the region were jubilant over Hamas's triumph and considered it as their own victory as well. Arab and Muslim regimes, on the other hand, have watched the rise of Hamas to power with worry and suspicion, fearing that its victory will encourage their local Islamists to pursue power more vigorously. Secular groups and individuals in the region have been divided. They support the nationalist liberation side of Hamas, but are anxious over its religious and social stance.

At the international level, a Palestinian government led by Hamas was regarded as a highly unpalatable fruit of democracy. The West in particular was caught in the dilemma of having to either accept such an undesirable result in order to show the Arab and Muslim world that its call for democracy in the region had been sincere, or be seen to cynically partake in an Israeli effort to bring down Hamas's government and risk losing any credibility.

HAMAS'S ECONOMIC OUTLOOK

What is Hamas's economic thinking?

Hamas has no distinct economic thinking or national programme that is any different from the 'free-market' basis that used to be the foundation of the Palestinian economy.

This economy has been functioning for years according to capitalist norms, although it is weak and fragile, because of crippling Israeli limitations and control. Unlike the Palestinian leftists, whose strong stamp of socialism colours their economic thinking, Hamas puts forth no particular economic ideology. Hamas as a party has hardly offered an integral vision of a so-called 'Islamic economy', which is sometimes referred to by individual Hamas figures.

By and large, the movement is content with the capitalist mode of economy which is based on free enterprise. It subscribes to the widespread belief within the circles of Islamist movements that Islam encourages free enterprise and enshrines the right to hold individual property. Therefore, the very basics of any 'Islamic economy' are close enough to the underlying tenets of capitalism. Yet the morality of such an 'Islamic economy' is closer to socialism. Many religious notions, such as a deep interest in justice and equality, obligatory systems of helping the poor, curbing monopolies and the prohibition of the unfair accumulation of fortunes, all echo the essences of socialist thought.

In practice, Hamas membership includes merchants, businesspeople and the rich as well as the middle class and poor. The well-off members have always been looked on with respect and admiration because of their continuous donations to the movement. Outside Palestine, rich Muslim businesspeople in the Gulf countries and other Muslim places represent the main source of Hamas's funding. Therefore, Hamas's experience of 'capitalism' and 'capitalist' people is somewhat positive. In recent years, however, there has been scattered criticism of the international economy and the monopolies of globalization, but these appear only in the margins of discussions of other major issues, such as the global hegemony of the United States.

In its attempt to secure a confidence vote from the Palestinian parliament in March 2006, the governing Hamas statement showed perhaps too much eagerness to emphasize its interest in encouraging foreign investors to come to Palestine and explore economic opportunities. Hamas vowed that:

> it would build the economic institutions of the country on foundations that will attract investment, raise the rates of growth, prevent monopoly and exploitation, protect workers, encourage manufacturing, increase exports, develop trade with the Arab countries and the world in general, and in ways that serve our Palestinian interests and strengthen our self capacities, by issuing laws that are appropriate for all of this.

GRASSROOTS SOCIAL WORK

What is the role of Hamas at the grassroots level in Palestinian society?

Grassroots work has always been Hamas's strongest aspect. Its unstoppable rise over the past 20 years and eventual triumph over other Palestinian factions is largely attributed to its success in social work. This work takes the form of providing structured educational, health and welfare services and help to the poor. Through powerful pervasive networks of charities, mosques, unions, schools and sport clubs, Hamas's assistance and care of needy people have been felt personally by hundreds of thousands of Palestinians. The provision of these services has also been marked by honesty and transparency, which equally has always been compared with the corrupt performance of other major Palestinian factions, particularly Fatah, which controlled the Palestinian Authority from 1994. The popularity of Hamas and its victory in the 2006 elections is at least partially an outcome of its sustained devotion to helping the poor. Hamas was known to give monthly help even to people who worked for the Fatah Palestinian Authority when their income was considered to be below the poverty line.

Known to be Hamas's major strategic strength, the Islamic charities and institutions run by the movement have always been targeted by Israel. For years Israeli attacks aimed to close down these charities, block their funds and mobilize international campaigns against their external donors. Israel has tried to claim that Hamas's social work organizations in the West Bank and the Gaza Strip channel funds to Hamas's military activities. However, the real intention behind the continuous harassment and closure of these charities and facilities, either by Israel or later by the Palestinian Authority, was the popularity they bring to Hamas.

After 9/11 the pressure on Hamas and its activities multiplied. Israel succeeded in mobilizing the United States and the United Kingdom to take measures against a number of Islamic organizations accused of sending funds to Hamas's charities. The United States also pressured the Palestinian Authority to act against Hamas's social activities, which included providing monthly stipends to the families of 'martyrs' to the cause of liberation, such as suicide bombers. This particularly was seen as an indirect encouragement for the future recruitment of bombers, who would rest assured that their families would enjoy protection and support.

At various periods of time Hamas's social work was really hindered or crippled by Israeli or official Palestinian efforts, yet it would gather momentum again and resume its operations. In the years 2003/04 the Palestinian Authority yielded to Israeli/US pressure and took harsh measures against Hamas's charities, including freezing the bank accounts of twelve charities in the West Bank and 38 in the Gaza Strip. The Islamic Society, with its nine branches in the Gaza Strip, was a particular target. Protesting against these measures, thousands of Palestinian families took to the streets in November 2003, throwing stones at the premises of the Legislative Council. According to local field workers, there were 120,000 Palestinians receiving monthly financial help from those charities. Thirty thousand more benefit from them on an annual basis.

Closing those charities did not help in either lessening Hamas's military attacks, or reducing its popularity. Despite all the ruthless measures against them, not only by Israel but also by the Palestinian Authority, these charitable organizations remained functioning, serving hundreds of thousands of poor Palestinians in the Gaza Strip and the West Bank.

At one point, there was a remarkable show of power by Hamas against the combined efforts of Israel, the United States and the Palestinian Authority to block Hamas's funds. Hamas wanted to show that it could solicit funds from ordinary Palestinians to support its organizational and military activities, and that it did not need to rely on its impounded funds, nor would any international blockade against external sources of funding destroy it. Thus, it organized a one-day fundraising campaign in the Gaza Strip on Friday, 9 April 2004. During and after Friday prayers Hamas appealed to the Gazans to donate to the movement and specifically to its Izzedin al-Qassam military wing (not to any outfit or charity affiliated to it). Canvassing all the mosques and public places across the Gaza Strip, Hamas collected huge sums of money. According to independent local sources, around US$1.2 million was estimated to have been collected on that day. Hamas's own estimate was more than double that figure.

Does Hamas's social programme include imposing Islamic symbols such as the hijab *and other notions of* sharia *law on the Palestinians?*

Ironically, within the sphere of Hamas's social work – its most powerful strategic asset – lies one of the weakest aspects of the movement: its heavily religious societal outlook. As discussed in Chapter 2, Hamas is a blend of liberation movement and religious party. The religious drive within Hamas is indeed visible and powerful, prompting many Palestinians to ask whether the movement would be willing to impose its own views and understanding of Islam on Palestinian society in the event of taking power.

Hamas's often-declared position is that it will never impose any religious practice on the Palestinians. Addressing detailed questions about the movement's stance regarding the *hijab*, alcohol, segregation between males and females and applying certain aspects of *sharia* law, Hamas's spokespersons are unanimous in negating the possibility of Hamas imposing such things on the Palestinians against their will. However there is a social dynamism and reality in the West Bank, and even more evident in the Gaza Strip, that reflects indirect practices or influences that contradict these official declarations. Because of the heavy presence of Hamas and the efficiency of its social activities, an atmosphere exists which has to some degree precipitated the indirect imposition of Hamas's norms on the Palestinians they support and help. Receiving continuous help and teaching from Hamas, many poor Palestinians would not only give their votes to Hamas in any coming elections, but in many cases would also adhere to the religious traditions and practice propagated by Hamas. And this does not simply follow out of gratitude or agreement. An unveiled woman for example would not think to apply for help from Hamas before veiling herself. This could be considered to be an indirect 'benign or paternal' imposition of practices.

More worrying examples surface, from time to time, of more 'malignant' impositions of practices. These include very direct and harsh interference by Hamas members against certain behaviour or events that are deemed 'immoral' in their eyes (partying, drinking alcohol, not wearing the *hijab*, mixed swimming and so forth). One infamous incident of this kind, which greatly embarrassed Hamas, was the murder of a Palestinian woman in her fiancé's car at the beach in Gaza in April 2005 by Hamas gunmen, and the beating up of her fiancé until he bled. Although Hamas condemned the incident and compensated the family of the woman, the justification provided by her killers was based on 'moral reasons and the fight against corruption'.

Hamas is still grappling with the idea of using power and influence to impose a 'religious moral code'. The more power and popularity the movement acquires, the more tempted it is to use its leverage to impose its social and religious ideals. There is visible confusion about Hamas's exploitation of its 'popular and political capital' on the 'religious morality' front. Some of Hamas's figures would convey the message with conviction that Hamas has the right to invest its 'resistance capital' in empowering an ideological social (or religious or cultural) vision on society. Not all Hamas supporters agree with its religious outlook. Palestinian society at large is very diverse, with secular and religious people, Muslims and Christians who have been living side by side for centuries without adhering to any rigid form of social or religious structure.

The potential misuse by Hamas of its 'resistance capital' in the religion/morality stakes is rooted in its self-perception of the role it has played. There is a valid claim made by Hamas that it has helped diminish certain negative phenomena in

Palestinian society, such as the use of drugs, as well as its considerable contribution to social services and aid to thousands of poverty-stricken families. Yet this has often been in tandem with propagating ideas like the sorting of the social fabric into 'moral' and 'immoral' classifications. Such potentially inflexible or divisive classification in the Palestinian case, and in any resistance situation, only complicates matters and makes things more dangerous, and pushes the national movement away from its all-inclusive character.

There is tension here between what pertains to 'resistance' and what concerns 'society'. Hamas is facing the same choice that many movements before it have done, of linking its social agenda (the Islamization of society) with its resistance programme. It should acknowledge that achieving the former goal might result in the loss of the latter. The experience of the broader Palestinian national movement shows that a pluralist national and social approach, which includes different moderate versions of religiosity, is the most successful in mobilizing the widest sections of the Palestinian people.

In the months that followed Hamas's control of the Palestinian Authority in March 2006, the confusion within Hamas's government on where to start and where to stop on 'imposing' moral religiosity is still apparent. The ministers of culture, media and women's affairs (all members of Hamas) have made scattered statements on issues that could involve 'moral imposition' and censorship, such as movies and the contents of plays and other material. However, it is early yet to build an accurate view on Hamas's government performance on this issue.

What is the position of Hamas on women?

Hamas is no different from other mainstream Islamist movements whose ideas and practices with regard to women draw on the experience and thought of the Muslim Brotherhood. This means adhering to a conservative outlook on women. It is an outlook that is not as narrow-minded and rigid as that of fundamentalist extreme groups such as the Taliban of Afghanistan and the Salfis of Saudi Arabia. But at the same time it is not particularly open-minded, nor does it match the levels of freedom and achievements that are realized by women in many Arab and Muslim countries. Specifically, women in the Hamas movement are politically active especially in universities and graduate sectors (with syndications of engineers, doctors and so forth). They have their own committees at local and national level, with their main areas of interest being the rather traditional spheres of women, charities and schools. Hamas's female activism reaches high peaks at the time of elections, when female members of Hamas are fully mobilized to reach out to Palestinian women and attract their votes. Whether these elections take place at the level of student unions or parliament, the power of the 'female voters' is paramount to putting Hamas in the lead. Thus, women are very central to Hamas at the level of functioning in the field and mobilization: that is to say, for Hamas's own political interests.

At other levels, mainly leadership, in Hamas women disappear. Since it was founded in 1987 not a single female has been elevated to a political leadership position, barring the late appointment in March 2006 of Myriam Saleh to Hamas's cabinet as (rather predictably) minister of women's affairs. The active female membership of Hamas consists mostly of university graduates who used to be leaders in their university years, but became sidelined after marriage and family life. Their role is limited to familial and social affairs that are bound by geographical areas. Compared with the broader Palestinian national movement, where many female figures have left a political impact at the public and leadership level, Hamas's women are almost invisible to the outside world.

The widely believed conviction amongst Hamas's male membership is that the responsibility of women is mainly to look after home and family affairs. This view is popular as a matter of preference, but not as a dictat that could prohibit active women from pursuing other paths in their life. Hamas women work in schools, hospitals, companies, the media and other sectors. But they stop short of pursuing leading political positions and avoid competing with men at those levels.

Within the 'resistance project' against the Israeli occupation, Hamas women play a significant mobilization role. They provide logistic and emotional support to the youth, and the mothers show a startling level of steadfastness when their boys are killed by the Israeli army. A very limited number of females from Hamas have carried out suicide attacks. Hamas leaders, ever adopting the 'benign paternal authority role', insist that they are not short of men to carry out these attacks.

When Hamas ran for the Palestinian parliamentary elections in the year 2006, it had on its list 13 females out of 66 candidates, with seven of them ending up winning contested seats. When Hamas formed a Palestinian government by virtue of winning the majority, it only included one woman in the cabinet, Myriam Saleh. To the disappointment of many Hamas supporters who were hoping that the movement would show more openness, the portfolio that was assigned to Saleh was the ministry of women's affairs, a step that in effect perpetuates the traditional view that women's affairs are separate and should be administered by women.

In more than one way, Saleh's credentials which recommended her to that post reflect the profile of many of Hamas's women: young educated females who divide their time between family responsibilities and organizational activism. Saleh holds a doctorate in Islamic studies and taught at Palestinian universities for years prior to assuming her new job. Married with seven children, she is a devout mother, yet very engaged in Hamas activities: she is the founder and head of several women's organizations in the West Bank. In her view, 'women represent not only half of society, but actually its foundation'. Responding to questions about whether the Hamas government will impose the *hijab* on Palestinian women, she said:

> We assure all women that we will not force anybody to wear the *hijab* … we only present our ideas by suggestion and with good intention. The majority of Palestinian women wear the *hijab* with full conviction and without coercion from anyone.

6 Hamas and the Palestinians

HAMAS'S POPULARITY

How popular is Hamas in the West Bank and Gaza Strip?

Hamas's landslide victory in the 2006 Palestinian Legislative Council (PLC) elections shows a clear measure of its popularity. The movement's election Platform for Change and Reform, along with four independent candidates supported by Hamas, reaped almost 60 per cent of the votes, with a turnout of 78 per cent of eligible voters. The victory stunned everyone, including Hamas members themselves. Yet, when scrutinized at a deeper level, the share of votes that Hamas won far exceeds Hamas's real power, and it merits closer analysis.

Over the many years prior to the 2006 PLC elections Hamas's results in all kinds of elections, including those of student unions, professional associations and municipalities, averaged between 35 and 45 per cent. The ups and downs in the number of votes given to Hamas at various times corresponded to the political environment at the time of the particular elections. When people have been more hopeful of movement in peace talks with Israel, Hamas's 'programme for resistance' tended to generate more doubt, and a drop in Hamas supporters followed. By contrast, when frustration with fruitless talks has been mounting and exacerbated by continuous Israeli humiliation of Palestinians, in such a charged atmosphere Hamas has tended to gain more support in any elections held. The level of frustration and anger among the Palestinian electorate at the time of the 2006 PLC elections was unprecedented. The conjunction of unstoppable Israeli arrogance and military aggression against the Palestinians, coupled with the failure of the corrupt Fatah-led Palestinian Authority, furnished Hamas with the extra support that was added to its original hardcore constituency.

Therefore, the 60 per cent victory that Hamas achieved in the PLC elections was not reflective of its clear-cut strength, but rather represented a coming together of two separate voting segments, what might be called 'genuine support' and 'conditional support'. Hamas's solid genuine popularity is the constant support that it enjoys regardless of the fluctuations of the political situation, either at the level of the conflict with Israel or in internal Palestinian affairs. The bedrock popularity of Hamas ranges between 30 per cent and 40 per cent of the entire Palestinian constituency. Any additional support to this share comes effectively from the conjunction of public reaction against the blunders and failures of Hamas's rivals, public frustration or outrage at ongoing humiliations from Israel, and most unforgivably, corruption within.

This assessment of Hamas's support was somewhat confirmed four months after its PLC election victory, when it had to face the first critical test regarding its popularity. Hamas supporters ran for the student union elections of Bir Zeit University, the biggest and most politicized Palestinian higher education institution in the West Bank. Historically, Bir Zeit University has been the stronghold of secular and leftist Palestinian groups. From the early 1990s Hamas started to fiercely contest the leadership of the student union. In April 2006 elections in an intensified electoral battle against the Fatah platform, Hamas won the largest number of seats, taking 23 out of the 51 being contested on the student council, leaving Fatah with only 18 seats, with the remaining ten divided among other factions. Hamas's Bir Zeit victory of 45 per cent of the votes is a much more accurate indicator of Hamas's real power on the ground than the inflated 60 per cent of the 2006 PLC victory, and is historically consistent as well.

How much influence does Hamas have among the six million Palestinians who live outside Palestine (in the Arab world, Europe and the United States)?

Unlike the situation in the West Bank and the Gaza Strip, there has been little visible presence of Hamas within the Palestinian communities abroad, barring the refugee camps in Lebanon and Syria. Although this situation could change after Hamas's victory in the PLC elections, it is certainly difficult to draw an accurate assessment of Hamas's 'outside' popularity. There have been few electoral processes outside Palestine with Hamas-affiliated groups partaking whose results could offer reliable indications of Hamas support and influence amongst Palestinians worldwide.

In general, the political orientations of the expat Palestinian communities vary according to their place and conditions of residence. Tentatively, it could be said that the closer to Palestine and the harder the living conditions for a Palestinian community, the more supportive to Hamas it could be. Also, the more the Palestinians who live in various countries are exposed to the influences of local Islamist movements, the more support they tend to show to Hamas. Thus, Hamas is notably popular in the refugee camps in Lebanon, Syria and Jordan. These are the places closest to Palestine, where not only does the daily 'hot news from home' flow in detail, but also these countries themselves unavoidably feel the pressures of the conflict constantly. In Jordan, in particular, where the majority of the population is Palestinian or of Palestinian origin, and the influence of Jordanian Islamists is paramount, Hamas's popularity matches the levels of the West Bank and Gaza Strip. As an indirect indicator, many Palestinians who are supposedly Hamas supporters typically vote for the Jordanian Muslim Brotherhood, whose average share of the Jordanian Parliamentary seats ranges between 30 and 35 per cent. The Palestine issue and support for the Palestinian struggle against Israel normally figure on the top of any electoral platform of the Jordanian Islamists.

By contrast, Palestinians who live in the United States, Europe and other places far from Palestine are relatively less supportive of Hamas. Yet again there is no concrete evidence that could be used to identify general trends for the extent to which those Palestinians support Hamas, or Fatah for that matter. Many Palestinians have been living in these areas since well before the establishment of Hamas, leading secular and non-religious styles of life. It is safe to suggest that the observance of religious teachings, which is indicative of supporting Hamas, is visibly less in evidence among European and US–based Palestinians than among those who live in Palestine or the Arab countries. Thus, Hamas's popularity within the former communities lags behind its levels within the latter.

How much influence does Hamas have on Palestinians inside Israel proper?

Inside Israel proper, that is to say outside the West Bank and the Gaza Strip, there are about 1.2 million Palestinians, who represent more than 20 per cent of the Israeli population. They remained on territory within what became the new Israeli borders during and after the 1948 war, and officially became Israeli citizens. Largely displaced from their original homes and villages, these Palestinians managed to resettle in less desirable areas within Israel, and have since suffered much discrimination, in spite of their nominal citizenship status. In terms of level of education, achievement, careers and freedoms they lag behind the bulk of Israeli society. Their inherent allegiance has always been questioned and they have been seen by the Israelis as a 'fifth column', working for the enemy. Their identity has been torn between officially being citizens of the state of Israel which was established on their own land, and their own 'Palestinianism'. Prevented from serving in the army or assuming high-ranking positions in the government, the 'Arabs of Israel', as they are usually called, have never been given the same privileges as other Israelis in relation to their political, linguistic and legal rights. Israelis look at them with deep suspicion. However, Palestinians everywhere consider them part and parcel of the Palestinian people. They live in almost exclusively 'Palestinian' cities and villages, with little mixing with the larger Jewish population.

Other than a minority of Israeli-Palestinians who have joined major Israeli parties, the politically active members of this community have created their own parties, spanning leftist, nationalist and Islamist leanings. These parties compete against each other in local municipalities to represent and defend the rights of Palestinians in Israel on legal grounds and without the use of violence. Since the mid-1980s, a strong Islamist movement has spawned within the 'Israeli Arabs', challenging all the other Arab parties. This took place almost in tandem with the emergence of Hamas in the West Bank and the Gaza Strip. The religious affinity between these movements is definitely strong, but they operate differently. The leaders and members of the 'Islamist movement' in Israel function in Israel within Israeli law, but Hamas functions in the West Bank and Gaza and is against Israel altogether. There are no organizational links between the two.

The 'Islamist movement' in Israel is morally and politically supportive of Hamas. During the 1980s and 1990s it was accused of being active in channelling funds to charities affiliated with Hamas. Hamas's appeal and activities have rained mixed fortunes on the 'Islamist movement'. On the one hand, Hamas has inspired its members to mobilize more strongly against the Israeli authorities, and to strengthen the 'Islamist' ideals within their constituencies. On the other hand, Hamas's suicide attacks in Israeli cities, killing civilians, have greatly affected them negatively, since, caught in the crossfire both figuratively and at times literally, they have felt unable to support Hamas publicly. At the high peak of the suicide bombings, leaders of both wings of the Islamist movement, which had by then split into two, publicly condemned Hamas's operations.

By and large, Hamas has little political leverage either on the 'Islamist movement' in Israel or on the overall Palestinian constituency there. Supporting Hamas would bring down heavy security and legal bearings upon the Arabs of Israel, thus even any emotional support they might offer is almost hidden. The most that Hamas can aspire to get from the Islamists inside Israel is support for its charities and campaigning against the deArabization of Jerusalem. Because these Islamists and the Arabs of Israel in general are official Israelis, they can move in and out of Jerusalem freely, thus they are able to mobilize themselves to protest about Israeli measures to eradicate the Arab nature and places of the city.

HAMAS AND SECULAR PALESTINIAN MOVEMENTS

What is Hamas's view of and relationship with the PLO?

The PLO was established in the mid-1960s and has since evolved to embody the Palestinian national movement. It is a secular umbrella of all Palestinian factions, left, right and centre, with the Fatah movement being its backbone and leading force. Established before the 1967 war and the fall of the West Bank and the Gaza Strip to Israeli occupation, the PLO was originally created to 'liberate Palestine': that is, the land on which Israel was formed after the 1948 war. Yet by the early 1980s the aim of the PLO became to liberate the West Bank and the Gaza Strip, and establish a Palestinian state with implicit acknowledgement of the state of Israel. In 1988 the PLO recognized Israel, and in the following years from 1991 to 1993 it engaged in peace talks with Israel in the hope of realizing its 'new' aim of a Palestinian state. When the Palestinian Authority was established on Palestinian territories in 1994 according to the Oslo Accords, the PLO officially became the ultimate representative of all Palestinians inside and outside Palestine (especially since the status of refugees remained unresolved). However the Palestinian Authority only deals with the Palestinians in the West Bank and Gaza Strip.

Hamas was bound to compete with the PLO since its emergence in 1987. It rejected the 'secular' nature of the organization and condemned its continuous concessions to Israel. In contrast to the later PLO conviction that Palestinian goals would only ultimately be realized through a negotiated settlement with Israel, Hamas advocated a resistance approach, which was justified all along the way by the obvious futility of the peace talks. Because of the secularity of the PLO and its 'capitulating' approach as perceived by Hamas, Hamas refused to join the PLO. Because of its immovabilty on this point, Hamas has always been accused of functioning at a distance from the collective national effort, and thus harming it. Not only that, it has been accused of undermining the PLO by not recognizing it as the sole and legitimate representative of the Palestinian people. Because the PLO fought hard against regional players, such as Israel, Jordan and Syria, to exact the status of 'the sole and legitimate representative of the Palestinians', it accused Hamas of indirectly undermining Palestinian legitimacy and representation.

Hamas, for its part, was inflexible on the issue of recognizing the PLO as the sole representative of the Palestinians. The most that it would acknowledge was that the PLO is 'a representative', not 'the representative', of the Palestinian people. Hamas also suggested that it might join the PLO if it was represented by 40–50 per cent of the PLO leading hierarchy. Hamas has continued to express its readiness to discuss joining the PLO, yet it has put forward terms completely unacceptable to Fatah, the central force of the PLO.

The Fatah movement has been fully aware of the challenge that Hamas has represented. As the PLO/Fatah continued its peace talks approach, almost from 1988 onward Hamas has travelled alongside with its 'resistance' approach. With the continuous erosion of PLO legitimacy because of the lack of success of the peace talks route, Hamas became more powerful and intractable in its rejection of joining the PLO. Finally, in 2005 Hamas and Fatah along with other Palestinian factions agreed on the principle of restructuring the PLO so that Hamas could join.

When Hamas won the elections of 2006 it dealt the greatest blow to Fatah and the PLO, this time challenging the status of 'the sole and legitimate representative of the Palestinian people' as it had never been challenged before. In its cabinet platform, Hamas refused, once again, to recognize the sole legitimacy and representation of the PLO, infuriating Fatah and many other Palestinians who have argued that the PLO is above factional rivalry. Hamas, however, was eager to form a national unity government and called upon Fatah, other factions and independent members of the newly elected parliament to join. They all rebuffed Hamas's offer partly because of its position on the PLO.

Will Hamas's rivalry with the Fatah movement end with an inevitable Palestinian civil war?

The rivalry between Hamas and Fatah has brought the Palestinians to the verge of civil war at various points between 1994 and 2000. Hamas's leaders, especially Sheikh Ahmad Yasin, were vehemently against such a development, and many Palestinians give them the credit for absorbing and defusing much of the provocations and suppression that Hamas faced from Fatah and the Palestinian Authority. The major issue that drove both parties to intense friction was Hamas's persistence in carrying on its military attacks against Israeli targets at times when the Fatah-led Palestinian Authority was trying to conclude incremental peace deals with Israel. Hamas's armed wing was seen by the Palestinian Authority as an uncontrolled group with illegitimate arms, which should be brought under the authority of the Palestinian security forces created by the Palestinian Authority.

In the post-2006 election period and with Hamas becoming the Palestinian Authority, Fatah attempted to bring down Hamas's government and started to play the role that Hamas used to play when it was in the opposition. While Hamas was anxious to buy time and bring calm to the Gaza Strip and the West Bank so that it could prove itself as a successful government, Fatah became the spoiler that Hamas had been in the past. The military wings of Fatah have always been difficult to control even by the Fatah leadership itself. With large stocks of arms and separate armed groups which move chaotically without clear focus and aims, the possibility of the Palestinian situation drifting into civil war is becoming higher than ever before.

What is Hamas's view of and relationship with the Palestinian left?

The left has a long and nostalgic history in Palestine, with the first Communist Palestinian party being established in Jaffa in 1921. It also had a pioneering role in inspiring parts of the Arab left movement in general. In the decades after the establishment of Israel in 1948, especially during the 1960s and 1970s, the Palestinian left was on the forefront of the struggle. Its relationships with the Palestinian Islamists and the Muslim Brotherhood during those decades were extremely bad. The Islamists were seen as a backward social force which contributed nothing to the struggle against Israel. When Hamas was formed in the late 1980s, the Palestinian left was confused about whether to welcome the sudden decision by the Islamists (in the form of Hamas) to become engaged in active confrontation with Israel, or to fear their definitely rising power.

Against this backdrop of historical suspicion and lack of common ideological ground, Hamas and the Palestinian left organizations developed rather limited relationships. They were mainly propelled by a collective rejection of Fatah's (and the PLO's) willingness to participate in the Madrid Peace Conference in 1991, and then in the Oslo Accords of 1993/4. Hamas and other Palestinian factions formed an alliance against Fatah, and fanned the flames of the spontaneous people's *intifada* in progress as the resistance alternative to the Fatah 'capitulating' approach. This alliance never came beyond the stage of issuing joint statements, and stopped short of any concrete joint political or military actions. Intrinsically, the Palestinian left rejected the 'religious content' of Hamas, and kept pressing for more secular emphasis in the struggle against Israel. In the end, suspicion and ideological differences overrode common cause and pragmatism.

One of the major issues that have kept Hamas and the Palestinian left apart has always been Hamas's unreserved refusal to recognize the PLO as the sole representative of the Palestinian people, as discussed above. The leftist organizations thought that this constant rejection revealed Hamas's future intention to exclusively control the Palestinian leadership. For its part, Hamas despaired of the left because whenever and wherever Hamas clashed on the ground with Fatah, the left would either stay neutral or implicitly support Fatah. Hamas has felt that the left have been hypocritical, only paying lip service to an alliance with Hamas against the political capitulation of Fatah. For its part, the left has always accused Hamas of short-sightedness and engaging in unnecessary political battles or field provocations.

After the elections of January 2006, Hamas's relationship with the Palestinian left have further deteriorated. None of the three small leftist groups which won seven seats in total in the PLC agreed to join Hamas's government. Hamas blamed them for foiling its efforts to form a national coalition government.

In March 2006, Mousa Abu Marzouq, Hamas's deputy head of its Political Bureau, publicly criticized the Democratic Front for the Liberation of Palestine for its refusal to join the government. He also predicted that this leftist group would disappear completely from the Palestinian political scene if it did not acknowledge the 'new realities'. One of the 'new realities' that Marzouq was pointing out to the DPF was the 'Islamic choice' that the Palestinian people had made when they elected Hamas, a choice which contradicted the DPF demand that Hamas state clearly that one of its government's objectives would be to 'secularize Palestinian society'. Marzouq insisted that it was illogical of the DPF to put forward this demand when it had managed to get only one member elected to the parliament (out of 132), particularly in light of the fact that that Hamas itself, with its vast majority in parliament, had not called for the 'Islamization of Palestinian society'.

What is Hamas's view of and relationship with Palestinian Christians?

In its conduct towards the Palestinian Christians Hamas has shown extraordinary sensitivity. Realizing that its views on non-Muslims and its dealing with them would always be brought under the spotlight because of Hamas's religious colouring, the movement has succeeded in establishing cordial relationships with Palestinian Christians. Bearing in mind that the vast majority of Palestinian Christians are quite secular in lifestyle, there have been in general few areas of potential friction with Hamas. It has been the convergences of nationalist cause, not the divergences of religious beliefs, that have governed the relationship.

In its official documents Hamas speaks with warmth about the sacrifices of the Palestinian Christians, who have shown steadfastness side by side with their Muslim counterparts in the face of the Israeli occupation and its atrocities. Hamas keeps referring with a deep sense of pride to the fact that Muslims and Christians and (pre-Israel) Jews have long lived in peaceful coexistence in Palestine, and Hamas would maintain that tradition. Also, the specificity of the Palestinian situation has compelled Hamas to adopt a consensual and cooperative approach towards other Palestinians regardless of their religious or political affiliation.

In actuality though, many Christians have felt uncomfortable with the increasing rise of Hamas. The religious atmosphere that is created alongside Hamas's political rise undoubtedly brings about a somewhat discomfiting climate for Christians, as well as for secular Muslims. There are some views and research which argue that the rise of Hamas in Palestine has put extra pressures on the Palestinian Christians, causing an increase in the rate of their migration abroad. But in general, there have been no religious-driven or sectarian friction or riots in Palestine during the lifetime of Hamas that could be linked directly to the movement.

Hamas's rivalry with other Palestinian groups has been almost exclusively politically driven. Its main concern has always been with the Fatah movement, which is predominantly Muslim. With the other two major, though smaller, groups – the Popular Front for the Liberation of Palestine and the Democratic Front for the Liberation of Palestine – Hamas has developed closer relationships, and both are headed by Christians. Indeed, this fact has never affected Hamas's position toward these two leftist factions.

In its 2006 election campaign for the PLC, Hamas supported two independent Christian candidates, one in Gaza and another in Bethlehem. When it had to form a cabinet, it included a Christian as one of its ministerial team. Although there are no organizational rules that prohibit a Christian from joining Hamas, the movement has failed to attract a single Christian to its membership. This failure embarrasses Hamas as it is the only Palestinian movement whose membership is exclusively based on Muslims, though not by dictat but by practical reality.

7 Hamas and 'International Islamism'

HAMAS AND MUSLIM COUNTRIES

What are Hamas's relationships with other Arab and Muslim countries?

Hamas's relationships with different Arab and Muslim countries vary from one country to another depending on various factors. These relationships exist at two levels; at the cautious official level and at the (usually) warm and more supportive popular level. In the Arab region, states that are known to have an outspoken, strong policy line against Israel, even if only verbally, are naturally closer to Hamas. This group includes Iran, Syria, Sudan, Lebanon and Libya, where Hamas has succeeded in establishing official links and has its own offices. Iran figures at the top of this group, openly supporting Hamas politically and financially, with Hamas enjoying almost full diplomatic status in Tehran. In the other countries, Hamas has offices and spokespersons and operates at the political and media level.

Another group of states includes Egypt and the Gulf states, Saudi Arabia, Qatar and Kuwait. These countries are well known for their non-revolutionary politics but they attempt to maintain a reasonable relationship with Hamas in order to counterbalance what is perceived to be the somewhat threatening Iranian/Syrian

[93]

influence on Hamas. Egypt is particularly keen to have strong links with Hamas, and has mediated several times since the late 1990s between Hamas and Israel to reach a 'truce'. Egypt's interest is in having calm and security in the bordering Gaza Strip, and to keep the rise of Palestinian Islamism under check so that it does not spill over Egyptian borders. A third group of countries includes reluctant countries who quietly consider Hamas to be a source of threat to their domestic affairs and thus an unwelcome presence on their land. Jordan and the Maghreb countries, such as Tunisia, Algeria and Morocco, could be considered among this group.

Beyond the Arab region, Hamas has established varying levels of links with Pakistan, Malaysia, Indonesia and Turkey. Delegations from Hamas make frequent visits to these countries to appeal to their 'Muslim brothers' for support for Palestine and for Hamas. Governments of these countries have established calculated links with Hamas in order to make sure that Hamas's contacts in their countries are not taking place behind the back of the regime. The principal concern in most Arab and Muslim countries is to monitor Hamas and its contacts and extract the guarantee from the movement that it will have no activities in the country, and will only be a receiver of support and not become an inspiration or mobilizer of any disgruntled factions there. However, in the cases of Malaysia and Turkey Hamas enjoys considerable contact and looks with high appreciation to the moderate Islamist ruling parties there.

In all countries Hamas's eye has always been on nurturing strong relationships and presence among the people, through the political parties and Islamic associations. The wider Hamas strategy is based on engaging Arab and Muslim peoples in supporting the Palestinians. Reaching out to these particular populations is vital, for it explains the Palestinian suffering and solicits support in moral, political and financial forms. At the official level, Hamas has focused on acquiring political and diplomatic recognition and legitimacy. Hamas has been very keen to be accepted as a political organization that is received and respected by governments, so that it constantly tries to mitigate its image as a 'terrorist organization'. Official links also help in enhancing Hamas's aspiration of representing the Palestinians and speaking for them, against the wishes of the PLO, the officially recognized body for that purpose.

At the popular level, Hamas has succeeded in creating strong local relationships with Islamist parties, associations and individuals. Not only within the realm of Islamists, but also within the anti-Israeli and anti-US camps, Hamas has enjoyed warm relationships and support. These relationships have played a fundamental role in helping Hamas in fundraising and mobilization of public opinion in the Arab and Muslim world. Supporters of Hamas will convey its message and defend its views and practices in their areas, by political and media means. The sympathy for Hamas in the Gulf and other Arab and Muslim countries often reaches high levels, creating the much-needed atmosphere in which Hamas's local supporters, organizations or individuals, are able to collect considerable funds for the movement.

HAMAS AND MUSLIM COMMUNITIES IN THE WEST

What has been the impact of Hamas's rise on the growing number of Islamist movements in the world, especially in the West?

In the general realm of Muslims worldwide, Hamas's rise as an Islamist Palestinian movement has encouraged millions of Muslims to further support the cause of Palestine. Muslim communities in the West are no exception. Palestine occupies a central and emotional place in the imagination and sentiment of Muslims. Hamas believes that with the adoption of a strong Islamic ideology, an additional level of power will be bestowed upon the call for support of the Palestinians. Ordinary Muslims would certainly feel more resonance with the Islamist discourse of Hamas than the secular discourse of the PLO. With the spread of Islamic political movements in the past three decades, Muslim communities in the West have become amenable to Hamas's call in particular. What Hamas has most wanted from them has been the propagation of the Palestine cause and funding of Hamas's charitable work. Almost simultaneously with the eruption of the first *intifada* in late 1987, many Islamic organizations were established in Europe and the United States in order to help the affected Palestinians. Money poured into Islamic charities that were efficiently run by Hamas. Hamas reaped the fruits and amassed further popularity.

In more specific areas, Hamas influences Islamist movements worldwide by offering a '*jihad* model' that is not controversial by nature of its just cause, but would not hesitate to use controversial means to serve that cause. Hamas's *jihad* is seen as directed against Israel, a foreign military occupation led by Zionist Jews against Muslim homelands and holy places. Because this particular *jihad* is not launched against a contentious Muslim regime or despised government where Muslims would end up fighting Muslims, there is a near consensus among Islamists everywhere on the righteousness and justice of Hamas's struggle. Also, Hamas is considered to be a source of inspiration – an example of steadfastness in the face of tremendous pressures – because of its committed refusal to bow to the status quo and international forces and recognize Israel, as the PLO did.

On the other hand, Hamas's controversial means, specifically the suicide attacks, have also influenced many Islamists and propelled many of them into adopting this tactic. Although they were originally introduced into modern conflicts in the Middle East by Shiat militants in Lebanon in 1982, against US-led multi-national troops, suicide bombings had to wait until 1994 before they were freely adopted by Hamas. Despite the justifications made by Hamas to legitimize this controversial practice (see Chapter 4), the movement partly bears the responsibility for having promoted this kind of self-killing amongst modern Islamists as a manner of inflicting maximum harm on the side of the enemy. It could be said that the waves of suicide bombings conducted by radical Islamist groups across the globe in the 1990s and 2000s have been greatly inspired by Hamas's conduct.

The activities of Hamas's supporters in the West have been restricted to informational, political and financial support. There purposefully has never been any military or armed action outside Palestine. Hamas has been vigorously strict on avoiding any direct or indirect engagement in armed activities in the West, or encouraging or approving any action in that direction undertaken by its supporters. As a result of this, many US and European judicial cases against organizations and individuals close to Hamas and charged with 'sponsoring the terrorism of Hamas' have failed. These organizations had been channelling money to thousands of poor Palestinians via Islamist charities that were associated to Hamas. All money transfers from the United States or Europe were undertaken via Western or Israeli banks, under the full monitoring of Western and Israeli intelligence as to where this money came from and to whom it was given. Hamas and its supporters abroad have been successful in maintaining a complete distance between the political, social and financial funding of the movement and its military branch and activities.

Is there either a visible or invisible presence of Hamas in the West?

There is no organizational structure for Hamas in the West. It has been felt that any such remote structure with any degree of party-strictness, however loyal it might be, would add an extra unnecessary burden on the movement in return for benefits that it already receives through the existing system of supporters. Thus, until the formation of Hamas's government in 2006, there was no official spokesperson or address for Hamas in any western country. In short, there had been no visible presence. Yet, as outlined above, there has been an 'indirect' presence through Islamist networks and associations in the West that have shown support and solidarity to Hamas either directly or indirectly by virtue of their broader support of the Palestine question. Many of these associations have been established by Palestinians who are driven emotionally and politically to support their people. Within these circles of western expat Palestinian societies and communities, more visible support for Hamas can undoubtedly be found.

What matters most, in an atmosphere charged by suspicion about Muslims and Arabs in the West, is that Hamas's invisibility in the West does not mean that it has an underground cellular network, armed or unarmed. Since it was established in 1987 and up to the present there has not been a single incident where Hamas was proved to have operated any illegal action within or against any Western country or citizens. The eagerness that Hamas has always shown about having a future presence in the West was specifically directed to, and restricted to, the establishment of official contacts with western governments. Succeeding on that front has always borne far more strategic significance for Hamas than recruiting individuals or setting up underground cells.

HAMAS AND ISLAMIST MOVEMENTS

Is Hamas part of a global network of 'international Islamism'?

The immediate answer to the question whether Hamas constitutes part of a global network of 'international Islamism', is yes – and no. If by 'international Islamism' we mean a coherent organizational structure, where various groups and parties worldwide belong to a single and unified 'umbrella' hierarchy, then the answer is no. If, however, the term denotes a loose common ground where Islam is considered the source of ideological convictions and guidelines, then the answer is yes.

Perhaps against the conventional thinking of many in the West, Islamist movements differ startlingly, one from another. First of all there are political movements and nonpolitical movements. The latter type of movement is hardly mentioned, as these function quietly and limit their efforts to charitable work, religious preaching and propagation of the call to Islam. But the other type, known as movements of political Islam, constitute a rising force not only in the Middle Eastern context, but globally.

Even within those groups affiliated to political Islam, the factors that separate them from each other perhaps override those that unite them. Some movements are engaged in fierce and armed conflict against their governments and are confined within their national boundaries. Their *jihad* aims to bring down these governments, which are seen as unIslamic, and to replace them with Islamic ones. Democratic means are rejected by these groups because they imply recognition of the non-Islamic status quo under which democracy is implemented. Examples of such political Islam groups exist in Algeria, Egypt and Pakistan, yet they are not the mainstream Islamists.

Other movements conduct their protests against the ruling elites in their countries by peaceful means, and in many cases through parliamentary political processes. The main groups in this category are the Muslim Brotherhoods that exist almost in every Arab or Muslim country. These groups abandon the use of violence altogether, and prefer long and patient incremental reform within the system. Each group operates within the nation-state boundaries of its country.

Another generation of more recent and radical Islamist groups is 'stateless' in terms of the focus of their *jihad*. This means they are not bound to the confines of any certain country, and consider the very existence of many Muslim states as an abnormality to the 'supposed' one and unified single Muslim country. These groups are the force behind 'global *jihad*', where fighting is driven by the injustices suffered by Muslims, and against those who inflict these injustices, regardless of time and space. The West in general and the United States in particular is the number one enemy to this type of Islamist movement. Thus, western interests in Arab and Muslim countries and elsewhere are their legitimate targets. Instead of fighting puppet leaders and governments installed by the West to maintain its interests in the region, they advocate that the fight be launched directly against the West, the principal culprit. 'By attacking the head, the tail falls off,' these factions are fond of repeating.

Within this mishmash of Islamist movements, Hamas is somehow unique. Its fight is not against any national regime, but against colonial foreign occupation. Its national liberation substance is no less potent than its religious creed (see Chapter 2). In many cases, and within the realm of 'international Islamism', Hamas's nationalist concerns have overridden its religious affinities. One recent and unmistakable example was its dismissal of calls from its 'Chechen brothers' to cancel an official visit of a Hamas delegation to Moscow in February 2006. For the Chechens, the Russian leadership is criminal and killing thousands of Muslims in the 1994 war against Chechny. Hamas, it was felt, as an Islamist brotherly organization should never shake hands with the criminals. Hamas dismissed this and thought that fostering relations with Moscow had far more value to the Palestine issue than showing solidarity with its Chechen brothers.

In conclusion, the concept of 'international Islamism' stops far short of any effective and concerted plan of action. It is only manifested in verbal solidarity, moral and perhaps material support, but does not amount to a coherent global force that would have any particular significance to Hamas.

What is the difference between Hamas and al-Qaeda, and is there any cooperation between the two?

There are big differences between the two movements, in terms of the ends, means and battlefield, and also the nature of each movement. Because of such differences, Hamas is indeed very anxious to keep itself well distanced from al-Qaeda, and certainly does not engage in any cooperation with it. If we compare the 'ends' of both these organizations, Hamas's aims are focused. They began with the 'liberation of Palestine' then narrowed down later and refocused on ending the Israeli occupation of the West Bank and Gaza Strip. Al-Qaeda's ends are almost the reverse in type: vague and without focus, and expanding, with the ultimate goal being to establish Islamic rule over Arab and Muslim lands after ridding them of foreign troops and puppet leaders. They also include intermediate goals such as forcing American troops to leave Arabian land, fighting US and British armies in Afghanistan and Iraq, and bringing down puppet governments in the Gulf countries and elsewhere. All along the way, al-Qaeda would implement a very strict interpretation of Islamic practices on any area and segment of any population it would come to control, with the Taliban 'model' as its ideal.

To realize its end, Hamas is engaged in a 'resistance programme' which includes armed struggle and political conduct. Within its armed struggle it has adopted the controversial tactic of suicide attacks, justified by the Old Testament as 'an eye for an eye', a stance that has currency it has to be said, in both Jewish and Muslim traditions. Yet Hamas's leaders repeat that 'resistance is not an end in itself', hinting that they would be ready to adopt a purely political strategy when the time was right. Al-Qaeda's means include armed struggle in all its forms. It engages in conventional confrontation against combatants, but also conducts suicide bombings, targeting civilians without reservations.

Hamas limits its fight to within the borders of Palestine, and its enemy is Israel. Al-Qaeda considers the entire world to be its battlefield, and although its principal enemy is the United States the list of its enemies is open-ended. It includes those European countries that took part in the wars against Afghanistan and Iraq in 2002 and 2003, such as Italy, Spain and Poland. It also includes Muslim countries that are seen as western bases, such as Saudi Arabia, Pakistan and Morocco.

Hamas has never targeted westerners either inside or outside Palestine. This is a strict policy by the movement that has been adhered to over years without a single exception. Al-Qaeda, by contrast, considers westerners as legitimate targets anywhere, be they combatants or civilians. Attacking the World Trade Center on 9/11 was the culmination of al-Qaeda thinking and practice, and demonstrates the extent to which al-Qaeda will go in implementing its indiscriminate strategy. The similar atrocities committed by al-Qaeda against civilians by bombing trains in Madrid and London in March 2004 and July 2005 fall far outside any thinking or strategy of Hamas. So would the targeting of any other civilian groups of westerners, such as blowing up tourists, hotels or residential complexes of western expats.

The nature of Hamas is also completely different from al-Qaeda. Hamas is a multifaceted social and political organization thriving within defined borders and parameters. The military provision of the movement is just one of its many other aspects. It is engaged in a political and democratic process like any other party, publicly and with very well-known leaders. Al-Qaeda, by contrast, is a completely secretive and underground organization. It almost confines itself to military activities without any political or social programmes. Democratic practices and peaceful means are ruled out completely.

Are we witnessing the rise of an 'Islamic and radical arc', starting from Iran, spanning Syria, Hizbullah and then Hamas?

When Hamas won the elections of 2006, Iran was on the rise, defying the United States and the world by enriching uranium, threatening to make the life and tasks of the US troops in Iraq very difficult, and supporting Syria and Hizbullah in Lebanon against US policies and allies. Iran was jubilant over Hamas's victory, and it started to talk about an 'arc of defiance' starting from Tehran, passing through Iraq where many of Iran's allies are, through Damascus to Lebanon's Hizbullah, and ending in Palestine with Hamas. This defiant alliance was meant to be against the United States and Israel and their arrogant policies in the region. In reality Iran's challenge to US policies in the region is tailored specifically to the US impasse in Iraq. While the vast majority of the Iraqi population and political and military groups would give loyalty to Iran in any confrontation with the United States, the Iranians temporarily enjoy a measure of leverage over the situation. Thousands of US soldiers in Iraq could be at the mercy of an Iranian decision to act one way or another.

Yet if the United States freed itself from the Iraqi dilemma, the situation could change and the regional influence of Iran could be circumvented. In all cases, Hamas would benefit from this 'arc of defiance' at least by strengthening its position and control of power for the next few years. One of the worst-case scenarios for almost all parties involved would be for Israel to attack Iran to prevent its development of any nuclear capacity. The repercussions of such a step are simply unimaginable.

8 Hamas and the West

HAMAS AND THE WEST

Does Hamas see the West as the enemy?

In general, Hamas's perception of the West is somewhat inimical. In common with prevailing thinking in Palestinian and Arab circles, Hamas holds the West – and particularly Britain, in the way that it handled both Zionist immigration in its Mandate-period administration and its pull-out in 1948 – responsible for the creation of Israel. This creation of a historically remote Jewish 'homeland' in 1948, in the heart of land that was and had been a solidly Arabic homeland for long centuries, resulted in endless troubles and an intractable bloody conflict. Hamas also blames the West, particularly the United States at the present, for continuous and unconditional support for Israel, at the complete expense of the Palestinian people, who are the only ones who seemingly have no rights in this matter. The West is perceived by Hamas, and by Palestinians in general, to be the staunch backer and protector of Israel.

Over the decades since 1948 western policies concerning the conflict in the Middle East have contributed to the cumulatively repulsive perceptions of the West held across the entire Arab world. Because of western support, Israel has acquired the mightiest military power in the region, including nuclear capabilities, from technology that was transferred to it in the first place by France and Britain, then by the United

States. With western backing and a population of 6 million, Israel has also enjoyed a vibrant economy, with a 2005 GDP of US$121 billion. That is very close to the total of US$128 billion for the neighbouring Arab countries including Egypt, Syria and Jordan, whose total population is more than 105 million. Israel had a GDP per capita exceeding US$22,000, compared with a mere US$1,100 in the Palestinian case.

Other wars in the area were seen to have been encouraged or led by the West to further weaken the Arabs in the region and maintain a superior position for Israel. The two Gulf wars against Iraq in 1990 and in 2003 reinforced the thinking of Hamas, and many Palestinians and Arabs, that the West is and has been stridently against any Arab military power that could ever potentially counter Israel's military arsenal. Hamas has also repeatedly pointed out the influence that Jewish lobbies have had on the policies of western governments, particularly in the United States.

On the Palestinian issue specifically, Hamas sees the western countries as never having exerted any serious pressure on Israel to comply even with the long list of UN resolutions on Palestine drafted carefully by the West itself. This list starts with Resolution 194 of 1948, giving Palestinian refugees the right to return to their lands and compensation for losing their homes and properties, and for being forced out of Palestine by the creation of the State of Israel in 1948. Other UN resolutions were made in the aftermath of the 1967 war. After Israel's occupation of the West Bank (including East Jerusalem) and the Gaza Strip, the United Nations issued Resolutions 242 and 338 calling upon Israel to withdraw from 'lands that it occupied' and rejecting the Israeli annexation of East Jerusalem.

The Palestinians and Arabs in general have felt dismayed by almost every single UN resolution on Palestine. These resolutions have been drawn up, as Hamas has often reiterated, by the western powers in ways that have always ultimately secured the interests of Israel in the first place. However, Arabs and Palestinians eventually accepted all these resolutions. The irony is that Western countries have shown a complete lack of commitment to the UN resolutions that they themselves have brokered, and no interest whatsoever in pressuring their prodigy Israel to implement these resolutions.

Thus, what shapes Hamas's negative perception of the West is not only the legacy of past biased western policies concerning the Palestine/Israel question, but also the current persistence in not changing these policies and doing nothing when agreed-upon resolutions are not upheld. Even despite this Hamas does not consider the West to be its enemy. In its literature and declarations Hamas keeps confirming that its sole enemy is Israel, and its battlefield is clearly limited to the boundaries of the historic land of Palestine. This has been a pragmatic position by which Hamas has avoided expanding the line of combat with its foes. Over years of acquired experience and maturation, Hamas's view of the West has become more sophisticated, and it is able to differentiate between various players and their different policies.

Has Hamas targeted westerners inside or outside Palestine?

Hamas has never targeted westerners either inside or outside Palestine. It has never considered individual westerners, or even western military and economic entities, as enemies or legitimate targets. The documented literature of Hamas as well as the record of events since its foundation attest not only to this strict policy but also to the ability of Hamas to uphold it. This policy is grounded firmly on two premises. The first premise relates to the above idea that Hamas does not consider the West either officially or practically to be an enemy. Therefore, westerners and western institutions and interests in Israel or in the West Bank and the Gaza Strip have scrupulously never been targeted.

The second premise is that Hamas distinguishes clearly between western policies and western individuals. It publicly and disparagingly criticises the West's biased policies over the conflict with Israel. Yet it has developed amicable contacts with many western organizations, experts, supporters and ordinary people. Hamas's leaders talk about people in the West as being kept in the dark over what their governments truly do against the people of the Middle East. They say that open-minded westerners who are keen to know about the situation in Palestine without prejudice would easily understand the justness and fairness of the Palestinians' complaints.

Hamas's ascent to power in 2006 has only enhanced its pragmatic policies towards the West and westerners. Senior officials, leaders of the movement and ministers of Hamas's government have all shown eagerness to open channels with the West. Despite the initial US-EU embargo against Hamas, its government has managed to defiantly survive that and to increasingly broaden its network of contacts with western officials and institutions.

What are Hamas's perceptions of western civilization and ideals?

Hamas's views on western civilisation and its ideals have basically been drawn from the somewhat entrenched school of thought of its mother movement, the Muslim Brotherhood. Its view is based on demarcating theoretical distinctions between the scientific, technological and administrative aspects of western civilisation, and its underlying philosophies and values.

Hamas, as well as other mainstream Islamist movements, welcomes what it sees to be the 'neutral scientific' advancements of the West, and faces no principled trouble in borrowing and using them. It refuses to countenance, however, what it considers to be the 'materialistic morality' of western modernity, and the lack of spirituality: the marginalization of the divine, and the secularization of humanity.

In practice, Hamas's dealing with, and de facto adoption of, 'imports' of western political modernity expose the relative infirmity of the theoretical distinction between these technological and non-technological aspects of the West. In the absence of sufficient Hamas literature on these issues specifically, Hamas's political practice shows that the movement is actually absorbing more 'western' values that it would like to acknowledge. Aspects of western-sourced political modernity have been consciously or subconsciously internalized by Hamas and manifested in its political, organizational and societal interactions. For example, the very nature of Hamas's liberation struggle has evolved on the nation-state concept (not the borderless Islamic *Ummah* notion), its party-based hierarchy follows the formation of political parties in the West, its internal affairs are run on western democratic practices, and its political rhetoric encompasses such western understandings as human rights and citizenship, in addition to the rule of the majority and the rule of law.

Many of Hamas's senior figures, and since 2006 Hamas's cabinet ministers, were trained in the West, or at universities that teach according to western methods. Hamas's experts in various fields such as science, agriculture, administration, accounting, urban and rural planning, education, medicine and engineering perform their expertise in ways that were originally western-fashioned. As can be seen with many other blue-collar Islamists, underneath the religious trappings and appearances lies a technocrat essence that is driven by the pursuit of perfection and self-interest.

HAMAS AND THE UNITED STATES

What perceptions do the United States and Hamas have of each other?

The US perception of Hamas almost reproduces the Israeli one. When Hamas first emerged in the late 1980s and early 1990s, there were signs of tentative, pragmatic soundings. Indirect contacts and messages were delivered to Hamas via US ambassadors in the region, or people around them. The stated aim was to closely 'explore' the positions and attitudes of the rising movement. In late 1992 and early 1993 the Americans had official contact and meetings with senior Hamas members in Amman, through the US embassy there. In those years, Israel itself was still hoping that the growing power of Hamas would eventually undermine the PLO and its main Fatah movement. Thus the low-key US 'exploring' course of action was indirectly approved of by Israel, insomuch as Israel hoped that the United States would influence Hamas to change its views and strategies.

But as the US/Hamas contacts themselves caught public attention Israel protested, and the US side abruptly ended them. Hamas denounced the US decision to cut off contact, saying that it clearly proved the deep-rooted influence of the Jewish lobby on Washington. Thereafter, the official US position hardened quickly against Hamas. Weeks after ending contact with Hamas, Washington labelled the movement 'a terrorist organization' in its April 1993 report on global terrorism. Initial discussions on whether Hamas was a liberation movement or a terrorist organization were prematurely suppressed within circles of policymakers in Washington.

Later on, and following Hamas's embracing of the tactic of suicide bombings on a large scale in 1995 and 1996, the official US position grew more hostile. Washington exerted enormous pressure on the Fatah-led Palestinian Authority during that time to suppress Hamas and dismantle its armed wing, a demand that always fell beyond the Palestinian Authority's capacity. Back home, US authorities banned the work of several Islamist and Palestinian associations and charities in the United States because they were accused of sponsoring Hamas. Politically, the United States threw its weight behind the Palestinian Authority, and saw no role for Hamas unless it would disarm itself completely, denounce 'terrorism' and recognize Israel. Hamas was not interested.

Over the next few years, in addition to their direct and bilateral assault, the United States and Israel continued to lobby the European Union to also proscribe Hamas. The European Union partly yielded and officially decided to consider the military wing of Hamas as a terrorist organization (see more below). The United States declared its 'war on terror' in the aftermath of the 9/11 al-Qaeda attacks in New York and Washington in 2001, and Hamas was further targeted. Pro-Israel neoconservatives in Washington lumped Hamas in with organizations such as al-Qaeda. In doing so they fulfilled Israeli demands to sideline the 'national liberation dimension' of Hamas, and relegate the movement to simply being part of 'global terror', although the differences between Hamas and al-Qaeda are many and unmistakable (see Chapter 7).

Washington faced the most difficult test concerning Hamas when the movement emerged victorious in the Palestinian Legislative Council (PLC) elections in January 2006. Hamas legitimately formed a government which was promptly attacked by the United States for neither recognizing Israel nor abandoning 'violence'. Ironically, these Palestinian elections themselves had been part of overdue democratic reforms that the Palestinian Authority had been pressured by the United States and Europe to undertake. The democracy that the United States had advocated in Palestine as well as in other Arab countries in the period preceding the elections had indeed brought Hamas to power. However, when it came down to it, the United States rejected the outcome of Palestinian democracy and mobilized an international political and financial embargo against the newly formed government. Succeeding in persuading the European Union to join forces with it, it stopped all financial aid to the Palestinians, bringing millions of Palestinians who mostly rely on the salaries paid by the Palestinian Authority to the verge of starvation.

On the other hand, the Hamas perception of the United States has also developed radically in response to the US 'unilateral war' on Hamas. It has just managed to stop one step short from considering the United States an enemy. The theoretical underpinnings upon which Hamas forms its relations with the world, and with western countries in particular, have remained intact, however. These stress that 'Hamas's dealings with foreign states and international organizations, regardless of any pre-existing political and ideological baggage, will serve the interests of the Palestinian people, their cause, and their rights.' The movement has managed to hold its official line on not attacking other states: 'Hamas has no dispute with any foreign state or international organization, and the movement's policy is not to attack the interests or possessions of foreign states.'

Hamas's government has followed the same line of policy and kept all channels and possibilities open for a new chapter, as a democratically elected Palestinian government dealing with the United States. The latter has shown no interest.

HAMAS AND EUROPE

What perceptions do Europe and Hamas have of each other?

In common with other Palestinian and Arab views, Hamas has nurtured a slightly friendlier attitude to contemporary Europe than to the United States. Europe also used to adopt a different line of policies about the Arab/Israeli conflict in general and the legitimacy of Palestinian rights than the United States.

Hamas looks at Europe as a diverse pool of powers. What separates individual European countries on major foreign issues, demonstrated in the lack of an effective common EU foreign policy, transcends what unites them. Thus, British, French, Spanish and Italian positions on Palestine and Hamas vary. These policies even differ from, for example, one Scandinavian country to another, Norway being a prime example of just one odd man out. Given this, Hamas has kept channels open and always pursued new ones with Europe. Both on the collective EU level and on the individual state level, Hamas has managed to have its voice heard in a reasonable way. Through European embassies in the Middle East, or through diplomats in the West Bank and the Gaza Strip, Hamas has maintained quiet European contacts.

Yet in September 2003 the European Union decided to denounce Hamas, while joining the US 'war on terror'. This decision implied that Hamas members, leaders or affiliated organizations would be banned from operating in any EU countries – something that never actually took place anyway. But to the dismay of Hamas and many European experts and diplomats, this pronouncement on the part of the European Union could only be viewed as European collusion with hostile US foreign policy as pursued by the neoconservatives. With that decision the European Union has effectively crippled itself from playing an effective role in Hamas-related Palestinian/Israeli affairs. In

[113]

particular, the European Union has jeopardized its pivotal role in brokering temporary 'truces' with Hamas, which it played several times during the second *intifada* of 2000.

The European Union has also been perplexed on other issues concerning Hamas. A major one is how to deal with the effective and widespread grassroots Hamas-affiliated organizations. On the ground, and apart from the aid directed to the PA government, multi millions of annual EU funds have to be channelled to NGOs for community projects, where the social-charitable bedrock of Hamas has been very efficient. It would be strongly questionable to fund only ineffectual and often corrupt non-Hamas-run organizations, while dismissing effective and transparent Hamas ones. This dilemma multiplied even more when Hamas won the majority of local municipality elections in 2005 in the West Bank and Gaza Strip. Municipalities are the main providers of basic living services, and have always been thought of as apolitical bodies that the European Union could deal with financially without sensitivities. When the social-charitable wing of Hamas took control of most of them, and in a short period of time showed considerable achievements, the European Union was further embarrassed by not cooperating with them.

Since Hamas formed its government as a result of winning the 2006 PLC elections, the European Union has faced the same dilemma but at an unprecedented scale. Hamas is now the official democratically elected government of the Palestinians, the address at which the European Union should be dealing. Unlike the United States, the European Union is looked on by the majority of Palestinians as more even-handed, humane and sensitive towards the suffering of the Palestinians, and less under the yoke of Jewish-Israeli lobbying. Thus, Europe has been shouldering a moral burden that materializes in the form of humanitarian assistance to the Palestinians, a burden which, it has to be said, has also been approved and acknowledged by other players, including the United States itself.

[114]

The European dilemma over Hamas was compounded exponentially in the April 2006 decision to suspend all forms of official aid to the Palestinians, pending Hamas's recognition of Israel and denunciation of violence. EU foreign ministers have approved a temporary suspension of US$600 million in annual aid to the Palestinians. Ben Bot, the Dutch foreign minister, voiced the justification for this move when he said, 'The Palestinian people have opted for this government, so they will have to bear the consequences.'

For its part, Hamas's government has resolutely refused conditional aid but has tried to tone down its militant discourse. It has strongly condemned the European decision, which it considers to be a collective punishment against the Palestinian people. The entire reaction against the Palestinian elections has been viewed by Hamas, and many others, as a scandalous exemplification of hypocritical western politics. An outcome of free and fair democratic elections has been shamefully rejected because the winners are not pro-West, or willing to accept or implement what has been imposed on them by their enemy, Israel. Hamas, however, has been able to do something of what it does best – exploiting the cracks and differences, in this case between European countries – to make some leaps over and around some of the obstacles of the EU decision. Again, quietly several European countries have acted outside the 'official EU policy', and are maintaining their channels and cooperation with the Hamas government.

Are we going to see Hamas members as Palestinian ambassadors in London, Paris, Brussels and Washington, among other capitals?

It is not a remote possibility that senior Hamas members will be acting as Palestinian ambassadors in western and European cities. The far more highly unlikely idea of Hamas having become the Palestinian government in the first place has already materialized. If Hamas survives the enormous pressures inside Palestine and the international blockade imposed on its government, all possibilities are open. In principle, the Hamas-run Palestinian foreign ministry has the discretion of appointing Palestinian ambassadors around the world. Judging from Hamas's past eagerness to cultivate its image and public relations, it should be expected that Hamas will reshuffle the current Palestinian diplomatic structure. Perhaps there are two reasons that will induce Hamas to do so. First will be the urgent need to reform Palestinian foreign affairs, in terms of both organization and message. Many of the present long-serving Palestinian ambassadors have run out of ideas and enthusiasm, especially those who have spent long head-banging years in their current posts – up to 20 years in certain cases. Equally important to Hamas will be the need to dispatch envoys abroad who are organizationally closer to the movement, or loyal to its political line. But once again, all depends on how successful Hamas's government will be in enduring the initial siege that it has faced in its early days.

9 Hamas's leadership and structure

LEADERSHIP

What does the leadership hierarchy of Hamas look like?

The leadership structure of Hamas is divided into two somewhat parallel but slightly dissimilar parts, one inside Palestine and one outside Palestine. The 'inside' leadership has always been promoted from the rank and file of the movement via internal elections, a practice that is well established within Islamist movements that have a Muslim Brotherhood background and traditions. The 'outside' leadership evolved differently because Hamas understandably does not have the same sort of membership organization outside Palestine that is has in the West Bank and the Gaza Strip. This outside-Palestine leadership was originally formed in coordination with the 'inside' Hamas, primarily as a back-up mechanism at the time the movement was formed in the late 1980s. It was plausibly thought that Hamas would need external support, financially and politically, and this was to be the job of the outside leadership in exile.

The strictly disciplined membership of Hamas is drawn from across poor and middle-class Palestinians, with a strong presence in refugee camps and most deprived areas. Many better-off Palestinians too give their loyalty to Hamas, in cities that are well known to be traditionally conservative such as

Hebron and Nablus. Members of Hamas in local areas elect their representatives to the leading party body, *Majlis ash-Shoura* (the Consultative Council) which is charged with outlining the overall strategy of the Hamas movement. This council in turn chooses members of the smaller 'Political Bureau' of between 10 and 20 people, who deal with daily affairs. The Consultative Council and the Political Bureau establish specialized committees that look after various aspects of Hamas's activities: charitable and social, educational, membership, military, financial, media and public relations, religious, women's and so on. There is considerable, if deliberate, vagueness on the exact chain of 'command and control' between the top political leadership and the military wing Izzedin al-Qassam. For security reasons, Hamas keeps ample distance between the functioning of each of its branches, and distances all of them from the military wing in particular (see below).

Hamas's leadership is effectively divided between three geographical areas: the West Bank, the Gaza Strip (both inside Palestine) and exile communities, largely in Jordan, Lebanon and Syria (constituting 'outside' Palestine). It is a matter of judgement which of the three enjoys more power. The opinion that the Hamas branch and leadership in the Gaza Strip is the most powerful has strong grounds. In general, the balance of power has always favoured the inside leadership. After Hamas came to power in 2006, the inside leadership was strengthened even further. But while it is safe to say that the two-branched inside leadership (in the West Bank and the Gaza Strip) controls the muscles of the movement, the outside leadership controls financial resources and external contacts.

Over the years, this three-branched leadership has managed to exhibit an astonishing 'decision-making management'. The challenge Hamas has faced in this regard has included not only shared decision making, but also day-to-day procedural management and coordination between the three branches. Hamas's spokespeople keep emphasizing the 'collective leadership' nature of their movement over personalities, and in practice they have shown a significant amount of adherence to this principle. As yet, there have been no authoritarian personalities or ultra-charismatic leaders who have used their influence to impose any individual vision on the entire movement, such as was the case with the PLO, Fatah and Yasser Arafat, for example.

How cohesive and united is Hamas, and are there radicals and moderates inside it?

Hamas is a highly sophisticated organization, with a coherent structure and strong culture of internal solidarity. It is the only Palestinian organization that has preserved its unity and integrity over the almost six decades of struggle against colonial Zionism. Since its formation there have been no splits or even small splinter groups breaking away. This is partly due to the religious values that encourage cohesion and disparage rifts, and partly due to its organizational background, which is rooted in the Muslim Brotherhood culture where members prioritize unity over contested views. Also, the challenges that have faced Hamas have fed into its united stand. Confronted by extreme Israeli measures since it was established, and then by a series of crackdowns by the Fatah-led Palestinian Authority since 1994, a sense of solidarity and purpose has only been consolidated further by all these security limitations and even arrests in neighbouring Arab countries.

Although Hamas has remained cohesive, the movement has witnessed the emergence of various and different views on some of the major issues. Moderate and radical voices have been markedly present at certain conjunctures, especially regarding the continuation of the tactic of suicide attacks. Some senior figures would project staunch positions on one issue, where others would use milder tones, leaving the door ajar for options and interpretations. The most important observation, however, is that there has been no development of any discrete group within Hamas that is geographically based, or politically or ideologically cohesive, that could be labelled as a 'radical' or 'moderate' faction. It is particularly inaccurate to issue a general description of the 'outside' or 'inside' leadership of Hamas as either moderate or radical, or to say that Hamas in the Gaza Strip is more radical than Hamas in the West Bank, or vice versa. Actually, moderate and radical voices do exist within all three existing branches of the movement.

Therefore, the dichotomy of radicals/moderates that some people try to apply to the outside/inside leaderships of Hamas, or to the Gaza Strip/West Bank Hamas, has little relevance. One of the reasons that Hamas has remained united is the inapplicability of that dichotomy to any geographical/ideological separation between its three branches. Had the moderate voices, or the radicals for that matter, overwhelmingly existed in any one of those areas, Hamas would have faced serious trouble and could have split up.

The cohesion and unity of Hamas has, however, faced the most serious challenge since its foundation after it assumed power in the elections of January 2006. Hamas has had to harmonize its organizational responsibilities with governmental ones under tremendous Israeli and western pressure, without losing the confidence of the people and with close coordination between its three branches. The challenge is extremely complex: top Hamas leaders inside or outside Palestine versus the Hamas prime minister, Hamas government ministers versus Hamas movement leaders, Hamas's external relationships versus the foreign affairs of the Hamas government, and so on. Power and responsibility will inevitably be fragmented, disputed and fought over, and keeping all that under control has required and will require extraordinary skills. Only time will tell if the united Hamas that existed before winning the elections will remain the same now it is in power.

What is the relationship between the political and military wings of Hamas?

The political leadership is the ultimate authority in Hamas. All other wings and branches are subject to the strategy and guidelines that are drawn by Hamas's Consultative Council and Political Bureau (PB). As mentioned earlier Hamas is multifunctional, and has separate 'agencies' to deliver its overall services and strategy. In relation to Hamas's military action it is the political leadership that decides whether at a certain period of time the military wing should carry on, halt military operations, increase or reduce them. Thus, the giving of a general green or red light is calculated politically and channelled through to the military.

At the same time, however, members of the political leadership repeatedly, and in all likelihood truthfully, claim that they know nothing about the specific operational technicalities of the military wing. For security reasons, Hamas's political leadership is kept almost in complete darkness about any detailed timing and places of attacks beforehand. So while the military wing functions virtually independently, executionally speaking, it is governed by a political strategy that is drawn and exercised by the political leadership.

A central question in this context is, if Hamas were to declare a ceasefire, is its military wing disciplined enough to implement it? Drawing on past experience the immediate answer is 'most likely, yes.' Previously, the military wing of Hamas has shown a great deal of discipline. On several occasions when Hamas's political leadership decided to stop military attacks for either political, security or strategic considerations, the military wing acted accordingly. In the lifetime of the organization there has been no rift visible between the two Hamas wings.

However, a major shift has taken place since Hamas became the Palestinian Authority, which was the administration that Hamas used to criticize and ignore when carrying out military attacks against the will and plans of that authority. Matters with Hamas-in-power are more difficult, and the stakes are now higher. More room has opened up for dissatisfaction and friction between the political and military wings. Having said that, for at least a year prior to its assumption of power Hamas committed itself to 'a period of calm' brokered by Egypt, according to which Israel would stop targeting Hamas leaders and Hamas would stop its attacks. After Hamas's victory it extended (unilaterally) that period of calm. Hamas acknowledged the pressure of other priorities which needed to be addressed urgently by the now Hamas government, and set aside the headache of military attacks at least until matters became clearer.

As Hamas has halted its attacks against Israel during its self-proclaimed period of calm, Fatah and other Palestinian factions have started their own series of attacks, partly to embarrass Hamas and partly in response to the unstoppable Israeli attacks which are also aimed at provoking Hamas. While neither retaliating against the Israeli provocations, nor matching the attacks of rival factions, Hamas's military wing has started showing signs of dissatisfaction and unrest. At the time of writing there has been no visible rift, but events are developing quickly and leave all possibilities open.

Hamas's worst-case scenario in this context is that its political leadership loses control over its military, or part of it. It is not unlikely that angry groups within the Izzedin al-Qassam military brigades of Hamas could split up into more radical and disconnected cells. This would be a really bleak development not only for Hamas but for the Palestinian situation as a whole. It could create an Algerian-like condition where the biggest Islamist movement splintered into unfocused and uncontrolled extreme groups.

Who is Sheikh Ahmad Yassin, the founder of Hamas, and what is his significance?

Sheikh Ahmad Yassin is considered to be the founder, the spiritual figurehead and the most historic figure of Hamas. Fully paralyzed in a wheelchair since he was eleven years old, the calm and charismatic leader was until his death the most popular personality in the Gaza Strip. At the age of 66 he was killed by an Israeli helicopter, along with nine other Palestinians, just after finishing dawn prayers on 22 March 2004 at one of the Gaza City mosques.

When Yassin was aged ten, in 1948, his family and tens of thousands of Palestinians were forced out of their homes and villages and driven to areas outside the 'redistributed' territory that would ever since be known as Israel. He and his family became 'refugees' in the Gaza Strip, where he lived a miserable and illness-plagued life. Despite his bad health he became very active politically and religiously. Sheikh Yassin was one of the founders of the Muslim Brotherhood in the Gaza Strip, as well as the founder of the 'Islamic Complex', an Islamic educational and charitable institution that was for many years the centre of Islamic activism in the area.

A schoolteacher by profession Sheikh Yassin ('sheikh', in

addition to being a formal title of address for a hereditary chieftain or village leader, is often and in this case used by the community simply as a mark of deep affection and respect) was sentenced to prison twice by the Israeli military courts, first for 13 years in 1985, then for life in 1991 on charges of directing military cells against Israeli soldiers. On both occasions he was eventually freed through deals. In 1985 Israel was compelled to free him with other Palestinian prisoners in return for releasing Israeli soldiers captured by Palestinian factions in South Lebanon. In 1997 he was freed after pressure by the late King Hussein of Jordan, who became infuriated with Israel for sending spies to Jordan to try to assassinate another Hamas leader, Khaled Mish'al, who was in the country at that time.

Sheikh Yassin was Hamas's main ideologue, mobilizer, pragmatist and populist. Projecting the typical model of a restless Islamist leader whose pragmatism never eclipsed his dreams of a principled utopia, Yassin's views and perceptions have formed to a large extent the political orientation of the movement. It was he who suggested the idea of *hudna* (truce), with which Hamas could reach a mutual ceasefire with Israel without breaking from its religious or nationalist principles. It was he who declared that 'civil war' between Palestinians was a 'no go' area. Even if Hamas was continuously attacked by the Palestinian Authority and its main Fatah faction, Hamas should never retaliate, Yassin insisted, because that could lead to internecine Palestinian war. At the social and religious level, Yassin accumulated rare moral authority in the Gaza Strip. He was a respected moral arbitrator and judge to whom families and parties in dispute could go and settle their differences.

Yassin's influence preserved a great sense of unity inside Hamas, for he functioned above the level of competition among the second-ranking leaders. But the very same unassailable position of respect indirectly crippled the emergence of innovative ideas and initiatives that could have been suggested by others. Other figures felt the need to stay close to Yassin's ideas so that they were not alienated by the wider membership because of their views. Even after his death, Yassin's legacy and statements are repeatedly referred to by current leaders and senior figures of Hamas.

Who are the most powerful leaders of Hamas?

Throughout Hamas's lifetime a number of names and faces have become familiar to the outside world as the main figures and spokespeople for the movement. In addition to Sheikh Ahmad Yassin, mentioned above, below is a list of people whose influence and roles are central in the formation of Hamas and its current politics. Yet before discussing these individuals it is helpful to say that Hamas leaders (especially those who are inside Palestine) project an almost common profile. The vast majority have come from poor refugee camps or the lower middle class; gained university education; belonged in their early youth to the Muslim Brotherhood organization either in the West Bank or the Gaza Strip (or abroad in the case of the outside leadership); spent a number of years in Israeli prisons; and either have been killed or have been targeted to be killed by the Israeli army. In terms of religious adherence, all of Hamas's leaders are deeply religious and conservative by the standards of ordinary Muslims. Their observance of Islamic teachings at the individual, family and societal level is visible, and it is a fundamental aspect of their personalities.

Another aspect that deserves attention in this context is the simplicity and modesty of Hamas's leaders and its senior person-alities. These virtues have always amassed great popularity to Hamas. The highest-ranking Hamas leaders still live side by side with poor and ordinary people. Sheikh Ahmad Yassin lived and eventually was killed in the very same refugee camp to which his family had been forcibly resettled when he was a child in 1948.

Even the prime minister of Hamas's government, Ismail Haniya, refused to leave his modest lower-class house and move to the comfortable residence of the former prime minister. In the first cabinet meeting of Hamas's government, which lasted for six hours on 5 April 2006, Haniya and his ministers had very simple *humous* and *falafel* sandwiches bought from the local shop for their lunch.

The cabinet declared that it would reduce by half all the salaries of the ministers and members of parliament, and would never pay them until all other Palestinians had received their salaries. The speaker of the parliament, Aziz Duwaik, another Hamas personality, refused to be allocated a special car with security and protection. He said that he 'will never cost the government budget an extra penny'. Likewise, members of Hamas's leadership outside Palestine project a modest style of life and conduct. For example, Khaled Mish'al, head of Hamas's Political Bureau, surprised other passengers in economy class during his trip from Riyadh to Damascus in March 2006. The Palestinian people compare this simple and close-to-the-people behaviour with the lavish lifestyle and arrogance of top leaders of the defeated Fatah movement and previous senior members of the Palestinian Authority.

The selective list below includes leaders from all three geographical branches where Hamas leadership operates: the West Bank, the Gaza Strip and in exile.

Abdul 'Aziz al-Rantisi (Gaza Branch, assassinated by Israel)

For many years al-Rantisi was considered to be the second in the leadership ranking after Sheikh Ahmad Yassin, the movement's long-time and spiritual leader. Al-Rantisi assumed leadership of Hamas in the Gaza Strip in spring 2004 after the Israelis assassinated Sheikh Yassin. Less than a month after that, however, al-Rantisi himself was assassinated. He was one of the founders of Hamas and a lifelong comrade of Sheikh Yassin. Charismatic and articulate by nature, he combined modesty towards his 'brothers' in the movement and toughness towards his enemies, which made him widely popular within Hamas and with Palestinians at large. He held hardline views but never contradicted Yassin's more moderate outlook. Secular Palestinian politicians and intellectuals were never impressed by his politics or discourse, however. He was perceived by them to be a master at packaging unrealistic demands in very powerful religious rhetoric.

Al-Rantisi was born in 1947 in a village near Jaffa. A year after that, in the wake of the 1948 war and the creation of the state of Israel, hundreds of thousands of Palestinians were driven from their villages and cities, including al-Rantisi's family, who ended up in the Khan Yunis refugee camp in the Gaza area. He went up through high school there, travelled to Egypt to study medicine, then returned to Khan Yunis as a paediatric practitioner. In later stages, he became a lecturer at the Islamic University of Gaza.

From his early youth he was politically active with a clear-cut Islamic leaning, and a member of the Palestinian Muslim Brotherhood organization. After the founding of Hamas, he was arrested several times, then in 1992 deported to South Lebanon for one year with more than 415 Palestinians. He was immediately jailed upon his return in 1993, and remained in jail until 1997. A year after his release, he was jailed again but this time by the Palestinian Authority (yielding to Israeli pressure) because of his Hamas activities. When the jail itself was targeted by Israeli shelling, the Palestinian Authority released him and other Palestinians. In June 2003 he narrowly escaped an Israeli attempt to assassinate him, during which his body-guard and a child passer-by were killed. His successful assassination a year later gave way to the rise of Mahmoud al-Zahhar.

Mahmoud al-Zahhar (Gaza Branch, foreign minister in the Hamas government)

Born in 1945, al-Zahhar is a veteran Hamas figure who became the foreign minister in Hamas's elected government in 2006. He studied medicine in Cairo, where he obtained a master's degree, then practised as a doctor in the Gaza Strip. During his early youth, first in Gaza then in Egypt, al-Zahhar became an active member of the Muslim Brotherhood. He was the founder of several medical societies and co-founder of the Islamic University in Gaza.

He has been known for a long time as one of Hamas's relatively moderate voices. At one point in 1996 he issued a rare independent public appeal through the media to Hamas's military wing Izzedin al-Qassam, asking them to halt their suicide attacks. Immediately, he was harshly criticized by members of Hamas and temporarily marginalized.

After the assassination of Sheikh Yassin and al-Rantisi he was elected as Hamas's leader in the Gaza Strip. He himself was the target of several assassination attempts by the Israelis. In September 2003 an Israeli F16 bombed his house in Gaza, wounding him and his daughter and killing his 29-year-old son Khaled. The house was destroyed and many other people were killed or wounded. The impact of that attack and the great loss of his son, combined with an increasing drive on his part to compensate for his lack of the charisma that his two predecessors enjoyed, led to Zahhar's stance and discourse becoming noticeably radicalized compared with his initial leanings. Yet when he became foreign minister he issued mixed messages of moderation and radicalism, and the more moderate Zahhar started to take over once again.

Early on, al-Zahhar was perhaps the first of Hamas's figures to talk about a 'pragmatic' interim solution to the conflict with Israel. In March 1988, four months after the foundation of Hamas, he presented a four-point proposal to Shimon Peres, then the Israeli foreign minister, which included the following:

1   Israel would declare its willingness to withdraw from the territories it occupied in 1967, including Jerusalem in particular.
2   The Occupied Territories would be placed in the custody of the United Nations.
3   The Palestinian people inside and outside Palestine would name their representatives to the peace talks in whatever manner they chose. Israel could not object to the choice unless the Palestinians also had the right to object to the representatives of Israel.
4   At a time agreed by both sides, negotiations would begin among the representatives concerning all issues relating to all rights.

Ismail Haniya (Gaza Branch, prime minister in the Hamas government)

Born in the Shati refugee camp in Gaza in 1962, Haniya has grown up completely immersed in the misery of the Palestinians who lost their land and ended up in impoverished refugee camps. His family was displaced from Asqalan near Jaffa during the 1948 war. Haniya finished his university degree in Arabic language studies from the Islamic University in Gaza, where his leadership fortunes were shaped as a prominent figure among the Islamist students in the early 1980s.

With the formation of Hamas, Haniya was at the forefront as one of the youngest founding members. After the first *intifada* in 1987 he was arrested several times, and in 1992 he was deported to South Lebanon with the 415 Islamist activists. Although Haniya was less visible to the outside world than the two above-mentioned senior members, he was no less significant. A well-known moderate voice within Hamas, Haniya amassed deep respect with the membership and great popularity within the broader Palestinian constituency. Sheikh Yassin, the spiritual leader of Hamas, appointed him as his first confidant and aide, and he remained close to Yassin until the latter's death.

Haniya is one of the most acknowledged moderate senior figures in Hamas. He was always the man who sought settlements between his group and its foes. During periods of friction between Hamas and other Palestinian factions, Haniya has always been seen as a moderator who is trusted by all parties and able to pacify volatile situations. His calmness and popularity, modesty and moderation led Hamas to charge him with the responsibility of leading its 2006 election campaign, which it won roundly.

Hamas decided to boycott the 1996 elections for the first Palestinian Legislative Council – which was set up according to the Oslo Accords signed two years earlier between Israel and the PLO – because 'they were an outcome of the capitulating Oslo deal'. Haniya and three other Hamas figures decided to run for the elections, in opposition to the movement's stand. Under mounting pressure, Haniya and his colleagues backed down and adhered to the Hamas official line. At the time, Haniya explained his pro-participation position to this author, which gives great glimpses into his political thinking. He outlined eight carefully written points that show the advantages of taking part in the elections, as follows:

- Participation in the elections will not amount to a surrender of Hamas's political position as long as the movement contests the elections under the banner of all the principles with which it is identified.
- Participation would guarantee a legitimate political presence for the movement after the elections, and Hamas would have secured a guarantee against decrees that could outlaw the movement.
- Hamas would be kept informed of, and be in a position to participate in, the formulation of legislation governing civil society that will emanate from the elected Council, thus securing a guarantee against exclusion.
- Hamas would be in a position to introduce significant and badly needed reforms in domestic institutions and could combat the spread of corruption.
- Hamas could participate in the creation of official institutions, something for which it always has asked, in keeping with its emphatic desire to participate in civil society and to promote internal development.
- Hamas would be well informed of developments in the final status negotiations and what is to come after that.
- Hamas would secure protection for itself and the institutions it has sponsored over the years, and its political leaders and prominent figures would enjoy parliamentary immunity.
- Participation in the elections would be a response to the demand of a significant number of our people who are looking for honest alternative and God-fearing candidates so that they can rest at ease about action in various areas of life.

Aziz Duwaik (West Bank Branch, speaker of the Palestinian Parliament)

Born in 1948 in Hebron, the West Bank, into a middle-class family, Duwaik completed his high school in the city, and then obtained three master's degrees in education and urban planning before he finished his PhD in urban planning at the University of Pennsylvania. In his early years he joined the Muslim Brotherhood then Hamas, and became a prominent personality in the city of Hebron. He was deported to South Lebanon in 1992 with other Hamas members for one year, where he became very well known as the English-speaking spokesman for the 415 deportees. After his return to Hebron he distanced himself from political activities, immersing himself in his academic professorship at al-Najah University, where he established the Department of Geography.

His almost sudden reappearance on the public scene after the election, when he was chosen by Hamas as the speaker of the Parliament, was surprising. Because little is known about his political qualities, some question whether he is really fit for the post. Others see his appointment as a smart move on the part of Hamas, who are bringing to such a high-ranking position a man with no enemies and a very well-known moderate and professional. Also, his appointment as effectively the third most powerful person in the Palestinian Authority hierarchy (after the president and the prime minister) has reflected Hamas's determination to maintain tight control on power. According to the Palestinian constitution, Duwaik would replace the president Abu Mazen should the latter become incapable of undertaking his responsibilities.

Naser al-Sha'er (West Bank Branch, deputy prime minister and minister of education and higher education)

Born in 1961 in Nablus in the West Bank, al-Sha'er is one of the new faces of Hamas who came to public notice at the formation of Hamas's government in 2006. He was an active member and leader of the Islamic bloc at al-Najha University in Nablus, before he left to study in the United Kingdom, where he finished his PhD in Middle East studies at Manchester University. Al-Sha'er has accumulated experience not only in political activism but also in the academic field and research. In the late 1990s he embarked on a course on religion and democracy at New York University as a research scholar. Before joining the Hamas government he served as the dean of Islamic Studies and Law at al-Najah University for five years.

Al-Sha'er is considered to be one of the moderate voices within Hamas. His training and travel in the West exposed him to the complexities of world politics and left a visible realist stamp on his thinking. From the Islamic perspective, he has written and published on various subjects such as human rights, the religious curriculum in Palestine, globalization, gender and familial violence. Unless he is sidelined by hardliners in the movement, al-Sha'er will be pivotal in shaping part of Hamas's thinking in the near future. By virtue of his strong background in Islamic studies combined with his modern understanding and sophistication, he could be in the position of theorizing new paths for Hamas in the short term.

Khaled Mish'al (Exile Branch, head of the Political Bureau)

Born in 1956 in the village of Silwad near Ramallah in the West Bank, Mish'al was displaced with his family to Kuwait after the war of 1967. He finished his studies in physics at the University of Kuwait, where he was an active leader of the Islamic bloc, which was the local manifestation of the Palestinian Muslim Brotherhood. In the late 1980s he became involved in the external leadership circles of the newly established Hamas.

[133]

Following the Iraqi invasion of Kuwait he and his family, along with thousands of previously displaced Palestinians, moved to Jordan where he started to become more known as a Hamas member and continued his Hamas external support. In 1996 Mish'al replaced Mousa Abu Marzouq as the top leader of Hamas outside Palestine, after the arrest of Marzouq in the United States. In Amman where Hamas's exile leadership was operating (only in the political and media areas as agreed with the Jordanian authorities), Mossad agents attempted to assassinate Mish'al in September 1997 but he survived.

In 1999 the relationship between Hamas and the Jordanian authorities soured greatly after the United States and Israel put pressure on the King of Jordan to expel Hamas's leadership, which he did in November of that year. Since then, the official address of Mish'al has been Damascus, although he moves constantly between more than one country in the region including Lebanon, Qatar and Iran.

Mish'al is the face of Hamas outside Palestine, charged with strengthening the movement's relationship with governments and outside organizations. In rallying support for Hamas among states and individuals both inside and outside Arab and Islamic circles, there are times when some stand at odds with the other; Mish'al conveys moderate and radical views concurrently, appeasing different audiences. Although articulate and popular among Hamas supporters and within Islamic circles, he is seen by others as lacking charisma and leadership sophistication.

Mousa Abu Marzouq (Exile Branch, deputy chief of Hamas's Political Bureau)

Born in 1951 in the Rafah refugee camp in Gaza, his family was originally displaced from Yebna village near Majdal during the 1948 war. After finishing his high school in the Gaza Strip he travelled to Cairo, where he obtained in 1976 a university degree in mechanical engineering, then moved to the United Arab Emirates for work. In 1981 he moved to the United States to continue postgraduate studies, and remained there until he finished his PhD in 1992.

Starting his Islamist political activism in high school then continuing in Egypt and the United Arab Emirates, his actual rise in prominence came among the Islamic societies in the United States where he headed several associations. By the time of the eruption of the first *intifada* in 1987, he had become very active in supporting and speaking for Hamas. Early on he helped in the establishment of the Islamic University in Gaza, and occupied a seat on its board of governors. Working behind the scenes he was free to travel between the Gaza Strip, Egypt, the Gulf and the United States, organizing the well-being of the newly established movement. In 1989 he reorganized the structure of Hamas after it had been badly affected by continuous Israeli crackdowns and arrests.

He moved from the United States to Jordan in 1992, when he was chosen as the head of Hamas's Political Bureau. His new position, however, did not deter him from visiting the United States several times for private business and political activism within Islamic organisations there supportive to Hamas. But he was arrested in 1995 in a New York airport, after Jordan's decision to expel him, and remained in a US jail until May 1997, when he was deported to Jordan. Hamas installed Khaled Mish'al in his place as head of the Political Bureau, and since his release he has been acting as Mish'al's deputy. In 1999 the Jordanian authorities decided to close down Hamas's offices there, forcing him and other leaders to move to Syria, where officially he has remained up to the present.

Abu Marzouq is considered to be a pragmatist. Operational

and a good organizer, he is reckless as well. His repeated visits to the United States in the 1990s exhibited carelessness and cost him dearly. He was also criticized in 1994 for what was known then as 'the Political Bureau (PB) Initiative' which was believed to have been his brainchild, offering Israel a solution that was based on the two-state concept, similar to what the PLO was calling for. Abu Marzouq's main points in the PB Initiative were:

1   The unconditional withdrawal of Zionist occupation forces from the West Bank and Gaza Strip, including Jerusalem.
2   The dismantling and removal of the settlements and the evacuation of settlers from the West Bank, Gaza Strip and Jerusalem.
3   The holding of free general elections for a legislative body among the Palestinian people inside and outside [Palestine] so that they can choose their own leaders and their real representatives. This legitimately elected leadership alone shall have the right to speak for our people's will and aspirations. It alone shall decide on all the subsequent steps in our struggle with the occupiers.

WHERE DOES HAMAS GET ITS MONEY?

There is of course very little public information about the finances or annual budget of Hamas. In recent years estimates have ranged from as modest a sum as US$10 million for the functioning of all aspects and branches of the organization, to as wild a projection as US$150 million. Perhaps contrary to the received wisdom created by the press, the smallest fraction of Hamas's budget is allocated to the military aspect. The lion's share actually goes to the social and welfare programmes that the movement provides to the Palestinians, especially the poor. These programmes, along with clean-handed administration and moral discipline, feed Hamas with sustained support and popularity among the Palestinians.

The sources of Hamas's funding, by the movement's own declarations, have been mostly donations coming from individual Palestinian, Arab and Muslim supporters of the movement. It is plausible to believe this claim given that neither Israel nor the United States has ever accused any state of funding Hamas, apart from Iran. Arab and Muslim countries, however, have been facing domestic pressure to support Hamas and the Palestinians, or at least to leave open the channels for popular support on a non-state basis. Thus countries in which potential individual or organizational donors are being targeted by Hamas for fundraising tend to turn a blind eye. In so doing the governments of these countries are trying to stand on a middle ground between strong local pressure to donate money to Hamas, and US pressure prohibiting direct state funding to Hamas.

Drying up Hamas's sources of money has always been a high priority of Israeli and US policies. Even funds that were clearly allocated for social services were targeted. The standard Israeli and US claim is that the Islamic social welfare organizations that are controlled by Hamas in the West Bank and Gaza Strip have been channelling funds to support the movement's military activities. In fact the real purpose behind these Israeli/US accusations is to close down these organizations altogether, to deny Hamas the immense credibility, political currency and appreciation it draws from them. Thousands of Palestinian families have been living for years on the monthly support given by Hamas's social organizations (see Chapter 5).

Hamas has also been successful in soliciting funds from wealthy and middle-class Palestinians in the West Bank and the

Gaza Strip. Challenging harsh Israeli obstacles and the American and western international surveillance of any money that could go to Hamas, the movement has prudently maintained local sources of funding. In hundreds of mosques across Palestinian cities, Hamas supporters donate money that ends up directly in the coffers of Hamas, funding its activities.

When Hamas came to power early in 2006, it faced the new dilemma of securing enormous funds not for its own functioning, but to feed the entire Palestinian population, who were stricken by increased rates of poverty and unemployment. A concerted Israeli-US-European effort succeeded in cutting off the supply of the annual Palestinian Authority operating funds that the previous Fatah administration had received. Their goal has been to bring Hamas's government to a complete collapse, and to 'teach the Palestinian people a lesson' for electing Hamas in the first place. In the eyes of most Palestinians this international blocking of funds is a punishment against Palestinians for having exercised their free will in the democratic elections that were urged upon them.

10 The new Hamas

HAMAS IN POWER, OR THE NEW HAMAS

In the first 20 years of its existence, the undoubted turning point in Hamas's political life has been its unexpected victory in the January 2006 legislative elections in the West Bank and the Gaza Strip. Bringing about new realities and challenges, the significance of these elections is tantamount to a paradigm shift not only in the thinking and practice of the movement itself but also across the whole Palestinian political scene. (See Chapter 5.) However, a 'new discourse' had indeed been showing up in Hamas's thinking during the campaign for these elections and has not simply resulted from their victory in the elections *per se*.

Demarcating the lines of 'newness' in Hamas's thinking, two significant election-born documents were issued by the movement: the 'Electoral platform for change and reform' upon which Hamas ran in the elections; and the 'Government platform' in which a victorious post-election Hamas suggested in March 2006 to other Palestinian factions a basis for a national unity cabinet.

In the 'Electoral platform for change and reform' Hamas incorporated the changes and experiences that had evolved in its organization over the past years, and showed how it had developed its perceptions, discourse and priorities. Measured against its original bold positions expressed in the early years of its inception, both in its Charter and elsewhere, the 'Electoral platform for change and reform' promoted an almost new Hamas. Yet drawing any conclusions about political parties based only on their electoral platforms can be misleading. Parties naturally try to draft their finest political statements at election time in order to attract as many voters as they can, and this electioneering rhetoric does not always reflect the real convictions and politics of these parties. Scepticism as a first impression is thus understandable when reading Hamas's carefully written 'Electoral platform for change and reform', where the movement clearly was striving to tone down its controversial views, broaden its national appeal and reposition itself at the heart of mainstream Palestinian politics.

Yet what largely offsets the rather legitimate scepticism about Hamas's positions as outlined in its electoral statement was a second document issued shortly after the January elections: the 'Government platform', which was issued by a triumphant Hamas in March, offering other Palestinian parties a common ground for suggested national unity. This document clearly presented the positions and policies that Hamas was prepared to implement. It differed from the 'Electoral platform' in its flavour of practicality and readiness to work with other Palestinian parties to achieve these practical goals. The pragmatism of this document, reflecting a Hamas now in power, clearly had overtaken the rhetoric of its 'Election platform' when it was running for the elections. Both documents, however, deserve closer analysis:

What is the content and significance of Hamas's 'Electoral platform' for the 2006 elections?

The significance of the 'Electoral platform for change and reform' stems from several aspects. First, it provided the political justification for Hamas's own change in position regarding the very idea of participating in any electoral process that was initially a product of the Oslo Accords in 1993/4. Hamas opposed those Accords and never acknowledged the legitimacy of any measures or structures resulting from them, including the Legislative Council and its elections. On the basis of this, Hamas refused to participate in the first round of elections for this council in 1996.

The 'Electoral platform for change and reform' for the 2006 council explains that Hamas's participation in the elections 'takes place within a comprehensive programme for the liberation of Palestine and the return of the Palestinian people to their lands, and the establishment of an independent Palestinian state with Jerusalem as its capital'. It reiterates that 'this participation will support "resistance" as a strategic choice accepted by the Palestinian people to end the (Israeli) occupation'. In confirming these principles in the preamble of its electoral statement, Hamas was anxious to make a clear distinction between its participation and its rejection of the Oslo Accords. Knowing this distinction would not be fully convincing for many Palestinians because the Legislative Council itself is indivisible from the Oslo agreements, Hamas raised the tone of its rhetoric and asserted that its participation constituted a form of its wider 'resistance programme'. At the end of the long 14-page statement, Hamas makes the even bolder statement that 'realities on the ground have made Oslo all but in the past ... all parties including the Zionist occupier speak about the demise of Oslo'.

Second, although the "Electoral platform for change and reform' reiterates the conventional canons of Hamas thinking and outlook regarding the struggle against the Israeli occupation, it does so in more nuanced language than previously. For example, there is neither talk about the 'destruction of Israel' – an eye-catching phrase that has been repeatedly used by the press to describe Hamas's ultimate goal – nor any mention of establishing an Islamic state in Palestine. Instead, the discourse of the platform focuses on 'ending the occupation', a term that cuts consistently throughout the length of the document. On two occasions this document borrows the language of old documents. The first comes in the preamble, which states that Hamas's participation in the elections is an integral part of 'the wider programme for the liberation of Palestine', and the second is mentioned in the first article, which confirms that 'historic Palestine is part of Arab and Muslim lands, and irrefutably belongs to the Palestinian people'. One could safely argue that these declarations are meant to sustain continuity with the old discourse of the movement, and represent more rhetoric than politics. This is fairly demonstrated in that the rest of the document offers no mechanisms to implement these goals, as is the case with other detailed and pragmatic declarations in the statement.

Third, in the 'Electoral platform' document Hamas gives considerable focus to the themes of 'change and reform', reflected as they are in the very name of its platform of issues for the elections. In fact it was rather surprising that Hamas, as a self-defined resistance movement with a military/jihadist outlook, chose such a mild theme and name for its election campaign. However, there was no lack of cleverness in concentrating on 'change and reform' against a backdrop of its corrupt and failed Fatah rival, and Hamas's electoral platform effectively relegated 'military resistance' to the back seat. There is simply no comparison between the weight and detail given to civilian aspects of governance promised by Hamas in this document, and the weight and detail given to 'military resistance'. Attempting to link the urgency of internal reform with the wider cause of the struggle against the Israeli occupation, Hamas stated that:

Change and reform will endeavour to build an advanced Palestinian civil society based on political pluralism and the rotation of power. The political system of this society and its reformist and political agenda will be oriented toward achieving Palestinian national rights.

Fourth, the 'Electoral platform' has significantly provided the broadest vision that Hamas has ever presented concerning all aspects of Palestinian life. Throughout the detailed 18 articles, Hamas left virtually no stone unturned in the societal and political setting of the Palestinians. It outlined what it would do if it won the elections in areas including resistance to the occupation, internal affairs, foreign affairs, administration reform and fighting corruption, judicial reform and policies, public liberties and individual rights, educational policy, religious guidance, social policy, cultural and media policy, youth issues, housing policy, health and environmental policy, agricultural policy, economic, financial and fiscal policies, labour issues, and issues over transportation and passage between Gaza and the West Bank.

Hamas has never before tackled such a wide-ranging spectrum of issues. Typically, Hamas (as well as other Islamist movements) has been accused of lack of pragmatic political vision: its rhetoric and mobilization override practical programmes and detailed perceptions. It is clear that this accusation was in the mind of the Hamas's members who drafted its 'Electoral platform'. Compared with previous pivotal documents issued since its inception (such as the Charter in 1988 and the 'Introductory memorandum' in 1993), this document has moved Hamas further into the realm of realistic politics, yet without diminishing the visible dose of religious and cultural mobilization that has been injected into it.

Fifth, Hamas's 'Electoral platform' also implied elements of what could be interpreted as its tacit desire, combined with quiet effort, to achieve the Islamization of society. These elements were received negatively by many secular Palestinians and others. Hamas persistently justifies this stance by arguing that these aspects reflect the true aspirations of society. Many people vote for Hamas at least partly because of these aspects, and the sector of Hamas's electorate who do not are fully aware of the presence of these aspects in the movement's programme, to varying degrees of controversy. Among these aspects is the confirmation that Islam is 'our frame of reference and the system of all political, economic, social and legal aspects of life'. Other articles stipulate that 'Islamic *sharia* law should be the principal source of legislation in Palestine', which is a conventional statement existing in the constitutions of all Arab and Muslim countries. In this clause and similar ones the point of controversy is over whether *sharia* law should be *the* 'sole and ultimate source', the 'principal' or 'one of the' sources of legislation.

In the articles that deal with education and social aspects, Hamas's 'Electoral platform' emphasizes that the values of Islam should be respected and included because they provide strength and wholesomeness to society. For secular Palestinians, an even more worrying statement occurs in the context of tackling cultural and media provision, stressing the need for 'fortifying citizens, especially the youth, from corruption, westernization and intellectual penetration'.

What is the content and significance of the Hamas 'Government platform', the prime minister's inagural speech to the parliament in which he asked parliament to furnish his cabinet with a vote of confidence?

Perhaps more important than Hamas's 'Electoral platform' is the 'Government platform' delivered by Hamas's Prime

Minster Ismail Haniya on 27 March 2006 before the newly elected parliament. In this highly significant statement, Hamas was addressing the entire world in new and carefully crafted language. Obviously, it was an audacious undertaking by Hamas to try to appeal to a host of completely different audiences. It had to live up to its promises and the expectations of its own membership, and to appease the wider Palestinian constituencies in particular, reassuring Fatah and other big losers in the elections. It also had to send the right and definitive message to Israel and beyond, that Hamas is not a belligerent and war-loving movement. The statement thus projected a moderate discourse with the hope of penetrating international (mainly US and European) audiences who were shocked and displeased by Hamas's victory. Concurrently, the statement had to appease and assure other Islamist movements and exponents of political Islam in the Middle East and beyond that the Hamas in power is and would be the same Hamas that they had always known. At the same time, it was essential that Hamas portray itself as a responsible moderate government, trustworthy to its neighbouring sceptical Arab regimes, which feared the ramifications of Hamas's victory on their domestic affairs.

As tedious a statement as it might seem to be, drafting the 'Government platform' was indeed an exercise in reconciling somewhat irreconcilable concerns and parties. Nonetheless, it has represented a true turning point in Hamas's political thinking. In it, Hamas has tackled the conflict with Israel in a language that is borrowed from international law and conventions. It focuses on the fact that the Palestinians suffer from the Israeli military occupation, and thus they have a legitimate right to resist it by all means. The entire thrust of the statement is confined directly and indirectly to the parameters of the concept of a two-state solution. There is no mention or even the slightest of a hint of the destruction of Israel or the establishment of an Islamic state in Palestine. It reflects very little inclination to radical positions and religious overtones. Someone who read this statement without knowing it had been produced by Hamas could justifiably think that it had been written by any other secular Palestinian organization.

At the beginning of his speech, Haniya makes a clear reference to the fact that his government will operate 'according to the articles of the basic law modified in 2003'. Referring to the 'basic law' clearly is extremely significant because this law was rooted in and developed on the basis of, and because of, the Oslo Accords. Legally and literally speaking, Hamas is functioning within the parameters created by the peace talks between Israel and the PLO, which it vehemently opposed.

The 'Government platform' merits a closer look. It stipulates seven major challenges that will make up the government's agenda:

> First, resisting the occupation and its oppressive undertakings against the [Palestinian] land, its people, resources and holy places. Second, securing the safety of the Palestinians and ending the security chaos. Third, relieving the economic hardships facing the Palestinian people. Fourth, undertaking reform and fighting financial and administrative corruption. Fifth, reordering internal Palestinian affairs by reorganizing Palestinian institutions on a democratic basis that would guarantee political participation for all. Sixth, strengthening the status of the Palestinian question in Arabic and Muslim circles. Seventh, developing Palestinian relationships at regional and international levels to further serve the ultimate interests of our people.

With the 'Government platform' Haniya called upon the international community to respect the choice of the Palestinians in electing Hamas, and to reconsider the initial negative responses to the Hamas victory. It also assured international donors who had been complaining about the corrupt management of the Palestinian Authority that any new aid would be spent in the right channels, and invited donors to establish whatever monitoring mechanisms they considered necessary to guarantee the proper expenditure of their money in Palestine.

On the United States and its position on Hamas's government, the document stated that:

> the American administration which has been preaching democracy and the respect of people's choices across the world is required before anyone else to support the will and choice of the Palestinian people. Instead of threatening the Palestinians with boycott and cutting aid it should fulfil the pledges that it made to help the establishment of an independent Palestinian state with Jerusalem as its capital.

Pertaining to the major rights of Palestinians, the statement stressed 'upholding the rights of Palestinian refugees to return to their homeland and for compensation, for this right is indelible and uncompromisable at the individual and collective level'. It also declared the government's commitment to work to free (8000 to 9000) Palestinian prisoners from Israeli jails, defend Jerusalem against Judaization and challenge all manner of collective punishments against the Palestinians.

On the peace agreements signed by the PLO or the former Fatah-led government and Israel, the statement assured 'other parties' that the government would treat those agreements:

with high national responsibility, and in ways that assist the interest of our people and their unchangeable prerogatives. It will also deal with the UN resolutions [on Palestine/Israel] with a high sense of national responsibility and in ways that protect the rights of our people.

The statement addressed at length, and with pride, the Palestinian exercise of democracy, and confirmed the government's adherence to that concept. It stated that:

as this government is a result of fair and free elections, it will adhere to the 'democratic choice', protecting Palestinian democracy and the peaceful rotation of power. It will also broaden the platform of political participation and pluralism because these are the guarantors of the sound functioning and stability of our political system.

It is noteworthy that this document, which was produced by a religiously oriented movement which has been seen to be cultivating its popularity on the basis of primordial allegiances, criticized all sorts of non-citizenship affiliation. It declared that 'the government would work to get rid of tribal and provincial loyalties and instead would encourage the concepts of citizenship and equality of rights and duties.' The notion of citizenship was emphasized as being the overriding one over other local, tribal or religious affiliations:

we will protect the rights of citizens and strengthen the concept of citizenship without any discrimination based on creed or political association, and will fight together against the practice of political or professional exclusion, and will struggle against [any] injustices inflicted on people.

References to 'good governance' were plentiful, covering a wide-range of issues:

the government will fight corruption and the misuse of public money and confirm transparency and fairness ... [and will adopt] new strategies to develop a public administration based on modern concepts of management.

On the economic side of Hamas's 'Government platform', free-market thinking is visibly expressed, yet with a close eye to social justice and care for the poor. But it starts by emphasizing self-reliance within the constraints imposed by the Israeli occupation:

our economic programme strives to achieve sustainable development through the release of our own [national] resources and by making the best use of our fortunes. We are aware, however, of the political restrictions and the effects of occupation that besiege our people and which have caused drastic damage to our infrastructure.

The statement then moves on to encourage Arab, Muslim and other business groups to come to Palestine and explore investment opportunities, promising that 'we will make available to them all help possible toward creating the appropriate investment climate including safety, economic protection and the issuing of necessary regulations'. It also stressed the role of such foreign investment as opposed to external donations, stating that:

investment is one of the underpinnings of sustainable development, where aid should not be relied on entirely, although this aid is necessary at this period of time. One of the utmost priorities of our economic programme is to encourage investment in Palestine, and our government will be actively ready to negotiate all the details that are required by foreign investment.

THE FUTURE OF HAMAS

Will Hamas be stronger or weaker in the foreseeable future?

It is safe to say that since its inception in late 1987 Hamas has continued on a rising curve. Certainly it has suffered setbacks and difficult times, but on the whole many successive conditions have simply fed into the strength of the movement. By analysing those conditions propitious to the sustainable growth of the movement it can be intelligently predicted whether Hamas will become stronger or weaker in the foreseeable future.

Hamas's continuing popularity and strength is intimately commensurable with the continuous brutality and humiliation that the Palestinians suffer because of the Israeli occupation and Israel's refusal to acknowledge Palestinian rights. Coupled with the impact of the occupation is the failure of Hamas's rival (secular) Palestinian organizations to deliver satisfactory solutions and means of resistance against Israel. Thus, inasmuch as these two blended conditions continue to define the Palestinian reality, Hamas will sustain its power and attractiveness within the Palestinian political and popular scene.

Both being in opposition and being in power bring Hamas

specific forms of good and bad fortune. When it was the lead-ing force against the Fatah-led Palestinian Authority up to 2006, Hamas enjoyed the advantages of distancing itself from the dirty politics of the Palestinian Authority, and instead offered alternative ideas on how to both confront Israel with-out surrendering and govern the Palestinians without corrup-tion. The more the Israeli measures continued to make the life of Palestinians hard, and the more the popularity and legiti-macy of the Palestinian Authority continued to diminish, the more strength Hamas was amassing. However, being in oppo-sition meant that Hamas was at the receiving end of continu-ous crackdowns by Palestinian security forces and military attacks by Israel. But if Israel and the Palestinian Authority succeeded at certain periods of time in crippling Hamas's military power, they were themselves crippled in their efforts to stem the rise of its popularity. Hamas's popularity and strength were not always joined hand in hand. A wane in its military strength would not cause a parallel drop in its popu-larity. On the contrary, successive (and successful) Israeli military attacks indeed weakened Hamas on many occasions but only served to increase its popularity.

Being in power Hamas enjoys more advantages, yet runs the risk of being caught off guard with many unfamiliar chal-lenges that could weaken its status and influence. As it assumed power in 2006 Hamas found itself for the first time in the driver's seat of the Palestinian leadership. Switching sides almost suddenly between opposition and authority, Hamas now has become the party that is asked to deliver on major Palestin-ian rights and issues over which it used to accuse its Fatah rivals of selling out.

Facing internal friction with the defeated Fatah party and external threats from Israel and the western world, Hamas's rule stands equal chances of failure and success. If Hamas internally succeeds in improving the living conditions of the Palestinians, particularly via a clean mode of governance, and externally remains faithful to the basic rights of the Palestinians in the face of Israel, then it will become stronger. Even if there is no progress on the front of the conflict with Israel, militarily or peacefully, Hamas will not be heavily blamed by the Palestinians. The dominant perception amongst Palestinians is that they have offered the maximum concession that they can by accepting the two-state solution, which even Hamas accepts in one way or another.

Yet if Hamas's government fails to live up to its promises, the movement will suffer in terms of popularity and political credibility. The extent of regression will depend on the factors that cause its failure. If they can be attributed largely to the movement's lack of capacity to deliver, then 'an exposed Hamas' marred with the tricks and games of politics will replace the clean and politically unstained 'utopian Hamas' of the past. If Hamas's breakdown in government is caused by external factors, however, the loss of Hamas's popularity will be minimal. It will simply return to the opposition side, but with more taste for power and the experience to make a comeback.

What will be the impact of Hamas on Middle Eastern politics and stability?

Making predictions regarding future politics in the Middle East is a typically futile exercise. Very much like moving sands, this area is marked by a mixture of heavy external meddling and internal vulnerabilities, which produce ever-changing formations of alliances and enmities. States, parties and political players in the Middle Eastern sphere can work hard and for a long time, and end up with nothing more than ironically having served the goals of their enemies. The United States allegedly presses for democratic change in the region, and when it happens, democracy brings to power anti-US parties. Israel becomes anxious and troubled because Hamas wins the Palestinian elections, but exactly since Hamas is finally in a position of political legitimacy Israeli citizens feel safer because Hamas has stopped its attacks. The fluidity and rapid pace of a seemingly endless series of major events allow for sudden rises, diversions or setbacks on the side of this party or that.

Accounting for any anticipated role and impact of Hamas in the future politics of the region is but a case in point. However, any predictions that are made will be as plausible as possible if they remain firmly rooted in the reality that has brought about a triumphant Hamas in the first place. This is a necessary, if not sufficient, prerequisite for any attempt at assessing the movement's role and impact at the regional level.

Reflecting the irony and juxtapositions mentioned earlier, it was ironic that many of the propitious conditions that led to the Hamas victory in the 2006 elections were created by its enemies and rivals. Israel and the United States had greatly weakened Fatah and the Palestinian Authority, and in so doing laid the road for Hamas's march to power.

Beyond the Palestinian and Israeli context, the region as a whole has been taking on a new shape. Although it is surely in the opposite direction to the one most desired by the United States, it was certainly favourable to Hamas. And if the war in Iraq was meant to reshape the region toward a new US-led geopolitic, Iran has emerged as the unlikely beneficiary of influence as a result of that US intervention.

After three years of the Iraq war, Iran has come to control key aspects of internal developments in Iraq and could be a major director of its future. The Iraqi shia, who are not only the majority of the Iraqi population but also the largest group on which the United States relies in the country, would support shia Iran in any confrontation with the United States. Iran could easily play them off against the US presence there and bring the whole Iraqi quandary to a bloody new phase. In the short term at least, the United States feels almost crippled by the Iranian challenge, yet it is aware that the fate of US troops (and the whole adventure) in Iraq lies at the mercy of Iran. Because of this sudden regional leverage, Iran has gone to great lengths in publicly supporting Hamas and pledging to compensate for any cuts in the funding of Palestinian aid by the United States or the European Union.

Iran also supports Syria and Hizbullah, which in turn are strong backers of Hamas for domestic and regional reasons. Facing mounting US pressure to leave Lebanon alone, Syrians have felt cornered and compelled to undertake desperate survival measures, including public support of Hamas (as well as exploiting the Danish cartoon issue) to amass pan-Arab solidarity.

Hamas in turn benefits from the Iranian rise, and not only because it could receive direct political and financial help from Iran. It also wants to use the threat of its strong relationship with Iran, however temporary its leverage might be, to entice Iran's rivals to give more help to Palestinians. Saudi Arabia, whose relationship with Hamas has always been cordial, if tacit, has become deeply worried by Iran's high-profile diplomacy, rhetoric and closeness to Hamas. Egypt is no less nervous. Along with Egypt and other Arab countries, the Saudis are struggling to prevent Hamas from falling within Iran's sphere of power, politics and ambition. Thus they are offering a diplomatic and financial hand to Hamas. Turkey too, with its moderate Islamists in power, feels that it is in an advantageous position to play a regional role, not only because its ruling elite has a shared background with Hamas but because of its friendly relations with Israel and the West.

With many players in the region pulling strings in opposite directions, gaps are bound to be created, and Hamas should have enough skill and experience to exploit them. As long as Hamas is kept busy in Palestine and is not driven by pressures to extremes, its role and impact on regional stability will be minimal and confined to the Palestinian-Israeli conflict. Hamas has never carried out any military activity outside Palestine. However there is always the slim possibility that things could change if the movement found itself in an intractable situation. As rare and surprising as it would be for Hamas to consider military engagement beyond Palestinian borders, Khaled Mish'al, the head of Hamas's Political Bureau, voiced a rhetorical statement that Hamas 'will fight with Iran anywhere if the latter is hit by Israel'.

If a wider military confrontation between Iran and the United States were to take place in the region, Hamas could be pushed to identify a new regional role for itself. If such a confrontation is contained, there are few reasons to think of Hamas activating itself beyond Palestinian borders. Within them, however, whether matters will either radicalize or moderate Hamas is largely contingent on Israeli policies.

The irony of the Hamas–Israel dilemma is that when Hamas is in power, Israel enjoys more safety for its citizens. To preserve its legitimate status and focus on the pressing internal agenda, Hamas has refrained from launching attacks against Israeli targets. But Israel of course is completely distressed by Hamas's control of the Palestinian leadership. If it were to bring down Hamas's government and push it back out of power, Hamas could easily return to its military position, and another cycle of reciprocal violence could arise.

What are the best and worst scenarios for Hamas?

Hamas's best scenario over the next few years is to prove itself in government as it has proven itself in 'resistance'. This would require it to meet a number of difficult challenges: securing enough funds from the international community for the smooth running of government, including the salaries of more than 120,000 public service employees; delivering on the most pressing hardship conditions facing the Palestinians, mainly economic conditions and security; improving the daily position of Palestinians face to face on the ground with Israel without compromising its main principles; and containing those armed factions who could make Hamas's life difficult by spreading chaos and fear in the Palestinian streets. Achieving all of this needs different Israeli, US and European positions than the ones initially declared against Hamas's government, or at least passive acceptance of the status quo of a Hamas government without any direct and concerted effort by these parties to destroy its rule. In this bright scenario, Hamas would not only keep its popularity and further its political strength, but also gain new political experience.

Hamas's worst scenario is to fail completely in the eyes of the Palestinians themselves, particularly if this is caused by factors that are mostly considered to be internal and not external in origin. This could happen if US and European pressures on Hamas were somehow compounded with internal Palestinian rivalry and fragmentation. To ease the external pressures, Hamas might opt to indirectly compromise on its main positions regarding the recognition of Israel. However, if this were to happen without a guarantee of substantive gains for the Palestinians, Hamas would lose greatly. If it took this line, then in order to maintain a coherent policy, Hamas would probably extend its moratorium on conducting military attacks against Israeli targets. However this would give other militant Palestinian factions the chance to outbid Hamas in this sphere, claiming that they are more loyal to the principle of resistance than Hamas. If this were to happen Hamas might try to confront these factions, and the worst of this worst-case scenario would be the instigation of a civil war.

If Hamas's failure either as a government or as a movement is perceived by the majority of the Palestinians as entirely caused by Israel or external western pressure, Hamas would be able to absorb it, if not capitalize on it. If such a failure was seen as Hamas's own fault, then the movement would come out of the 'being in power' experience wounded and weaker than when it entered it.

The success or failure of Hamas as a government will be mostly determined by two factors: internal challenges posed by Fatah military wings, and external funding of the government. Fatah has penetrated the Palestinian multi-headed security forces, which belong to the Palestinian Authority, both before and after Hamas's coming to power. Fatah's own unreined armed factions caused trouble enough in the West Bank and the Gaza Strip for the Fatah-led government: it can be imagined what they could cause to a Hamas-led one. There is a great sense of shock and disbelief amongst Fatah's rank and file that their government no longer leads the Palestinian people. They feel that Hamas's years, if not months, are numbered; that this is merely a gloomy interregnum which will pass quickly, after which Fatah will return to power 'as usual'. The extent to which Hamas will succeed or fail in dealing with this challenge will greatly affect its fortunes.

The funding of the Palestinian government (of at least US$1.2 billion annually) is central to Hamas's success or failure in government. There has been a concerted effort by Israel, the United States and the European Union to cut off any foreign aid to Hamas's government. The United States has pressured Arab and Islamic countries not to replace western money in order to keep Hamas stretched to an extreme. They hope that by keeping enormous pressure on it, Hamas will be cornered by the mounting and pressing daily needs of the Palestinian people, leading it to yield to Israeli/western demands: to recognize Israel and denounce violence.

It is doubtful that this policy of pressure will foil Hamas. Rather, it could backfire badly. In the first place, the pretext for withholding aid – that any money going to the Hamas-led government could be used for 'terrorism' – is hollow and naive. Close knowledge of the movement will make it clear that Hamas – in its role as a militant movement, not as a government – has never been short of money to keep its own organizational functions running smoothly. Even during its most difficult times, when a combination of foreign intelligences kept a close eye on the channelling of Hamas's funds, the movement managed to survive. Now, with its popularity reaching unprecedented peaks in Palestine, it will keep receiving considerable funds from Palestinians both inside and outside Palestine, and from many Arabs and Muslims across the world as well. Hamas would face no problem in soliciting funds and donations to its own private accounts. But what Hamas requires to maintain its private operational affairs is very little compared with the massive amounts required to supply the needs of the entire Palestinian people, particularly the huge populations of economically devastated refugees. With the western blockage of Palestinian aid it would be ordinary Palestinians who would be deprived of aid and services, and not Hamas.

What would result from any western blockage of funds is that angry and frustrated Palestinians would become closer to Hamas as a movement, even though it might collapse as a government. Particularly following its democratic and completely legitimate election, Hamas would be seen in the eyes of the Palestinian people as striving to do its best despite all the moving of the goalposts and 'conspiracies' by the West and Israel. If any western obstruction of funding brought the Hamas government down, Hamas would be elevated to the status of a persecuted martyr, and the Hamas movement would simply resume its militant pre-election position, taking up arms and fighting back.

Recommended reading

Abboud, Edward. *Invisible Enemy: Israel, Politics, Media, and American Culture* (Columbus, Ohio: Vox Publishing, 1997).

Abu El-Haj, Nadi. *Facts on the Ground: Archaeological Practice and Territorial Self-Fashioning in Israeli Society* (Chicago: University of Chicago Press, 2001).

Agha, Hussein and Khalidi, Ahmad S. *A Framework for a Palestinian Security Doctrine* (London: Chatham House, 2006).

Aruri, Naseer. *Palestinian Refugees: The Right of Return* (London: Pluto Press, 2001).

—— *Dishonest Broker: The U.S. role in Israel and Palestine* (Cambridge, Mass.: South End Press, 2003).

Bishara, Marwan. *Palestine/Israel: Peace or apartheid* (London, New York: Zed Books, 2001).

Christison, Kathleen. *Perceptions of Palestine: Their influence on U.S. Middle East policy* (Berkeley, Los Angeles, London: University of California Press, 1999).

Davis, Uri. *Apartheid Israel: Possibilities for the struggle within* (London and New York: Zed Books, 2003).

El-Awaisi, Abd Al-Fattah Muhammad. *The Muslim Brothers and the Palestine Question 1928–1947* (London, New York: Tauris Academic Studies: 1998).

Esposito, John L. *The Islamic Threat: Myth or reality?* (Oxford: Oxford University Press, 1992).

Gee, John R. *Unequal Conflict: The Palestinians and Israel* (London: Pluto Press, 1998).

Gerges, A. Fawaz. *America and Political Islam: Clash of cultures or clash of interests?* (Cambridge UK: Cambridge University Press, 1999).

Helmick, Raymond G. *Negotiating Outside the Law: Why Camp David failed* (London: Pluto Press, 2004).

Hroub, Khaled. *Hamas: Political Thought and Practice* (Washington DC: Institute of Palestine Studies, 2000).

International Crisis Group. 'Islamic social welfare activism in the occupied Palestinian Territories: a legitimate target?' *Middle East Report*, no. 13, 2

April 2003.
[Online] www.crisisgroup.org/home/index.cfm?id=1662&l=1
—— 'Dealing with Hamas', *Middle East Report* no. 21, 26 January 2004.
[Online] www.crisisgroup.org/home/index. cfm?id=2488&l=1
—— 'Enter Hamas: the challenges of political integration', *Middle East Report*, no. 49, 18 January 2006.
[Online] www.crisisgroup.org/home/index.cfm?id=3886&l=1
Karmi, Ghada and Cotran, Eugene. *The Palestinian Exodus 1948–1998* (London: Ithaca Press, 1999).
Khalidi, Rashid. *Palestinian Identity: The construction of modern national consciousness* (New York, Columbia University Press, 1997).
Khan, Mushtaq Husain (ed.) *State Formation in Palestine: Viability and governance during a social transformation* (London: RoutledgeCurzon, 2004).
Malley, Robert and Agah, Hussein. 'Camp David: tragedy of errors', *New York Review of Books*, 9 August 2001.
Milton-Edwards, Beverly. *Islamic Politics in Palestine* (London, New York: I. B. Tauris, 1996).
Nafi, Bashir M. *Arabism, Islamism and the Palestine Question 1908–1941* (Reading, UK: Ithaca Press, 1998).
Piscatori, James P. *Islam in the Political Process* (Cambridge UK: Cambridge University Press, 1983).
Rogan, Eugene L. and Shlaim, Avi. *The War for Palestine: Rewriting the history of 1948* (Cambridge, UK: Cambridge University Press, 2001).
Saad-Ghorayeb, Amal. *Hizbu'llah: Politics and religion* (London: Pluto Press, 2002).
Said, Edward. S. *The Question of Palestine* (London: Vintage, 1992).
Sayigh, Yezid. *Armed Struggle and the Search for State: The Palestinian National Movement, 1949–1993* (Oxford: Oxford University Press, 1997).
Segal, Rafi and Weizman, Eyal. *A Civilian Occupation: The politics of Israeli architecture* (London: Verso, 2003).
Sha'ban, Fuad. *For Zion's Sake: The Judeo-Christian tradition in American culture* (London: Pluto Press, 2005).
Shlaim, Avi. *The Iron Wall: Israel and the Arab world* (New York, London: W. W. Norton, 2000).
Sontag, Deborah. 'Quest for Middle East peace: how and why it failed?' *New York Times*, 26 July 2001.
Usher, Graham. *Dispatches from Palestine: The rise and fall of the Oslo peace process* (London: Pluto Press, 1999).
Yousef, Ahmad. *American Muslims: A community under siege* (Virginia: USAR Publishing Group, 2004).

Index

violence
legitimate targets, 8
as means to Islamist ends, 8

wars
Gulf, 101, 02, 103, 106, 134, 153
of 1967, 6, 9, 106, 129, 133
World War I, 3
World War II, 4, 32
West Bank, 36, 39, 45, 46, 47, 48,
53, 73, 81, 82, 85, 87, 106, 118,
136, 137, 142, 157
annexed to Jordan, 9
fragmentation of, 60–1
Israeli annexation of, 6, 10, 19

military resources in, 49
social role of Hamas in, 19

Yassin, Sheikh Ahmad, 11, 13, 18,
49, 53, 56, 87, 123–5, 127, 128,
130
al-Yazuri, Ibrahim, 13
Yemen, 7

al-Zahhar, Mahmoud, 40, 128–9
Zionism, 3, 4, 5, 9, 24–5, 32, 33, 96,
105, 119
distinguished by Hamas from
Jewishness, 34